Self Compassion

Kindness to Yourself and Achieve Your Goals

(Start Self-kindness and Learn to Be Your Own Best Friend)

William Martin

Published By **Darby Connor**

William Martin

All Rights Reserved

Self Compassion: Kindness to Yourself and Achieve Your Goals (Start Self-kindness and Learn to Be Your Own Best Friend)

ISBN 978-0-9950956-2-5

No part of this guidebook shall be reproduced in any form without permission in writing from the publisher except in the case of brief quotations embodied in critical articles or reviews.

Legal & Disclaimer

The information contained in this book is not designed to replace or take the place of any form of medicine or professional medical advice. The information in this book has been provided for educational & entertainment purposes only.

The information contained in this book has been compiled from sources deemed reliable, and it is accurate to the best of the Author's knowledge; however, the Author cannot guarantee its accuracy and validity and cannot be held liable for any errors or omissions. Changes are periodically made to this book. You must consult your doctor or get professional medical advice before using any of the suggested remedies, techniques, or information in this book.

Upon using the information contained in this book, you agree to hold harmless the Author from and against any damages, costs, and expenses, including any legal fees potentially resulting from the application of any of the information provided by this guide. This disclaimer applies to any damages or injury caused by the use and application, whether directly or indirectly, of any advice or information presented, whether for breach of contract, tort, negligence, personal injury, criminal intent, or under any other cause of action.

You agree to accept all risks of using the information presented inside this book. You need to consult a professional medical practitioner in order to ensure you are both able and healthy enough to participate in this program.

Table Of Contents

Chapter 1: Self-Confidence 1

Chapter 2: Grasping the Evolutionary Advantage............................. 15

Chapter 3: The Role of Compassion and the Psychology of Shame 34

Chapter 4: What Compassion Is Not 46

Chapter 5: Mindset and Personal Growth 49

Chapter 6: Mindset as Binding to Compassion 51

Chapter 7: Mindfulness.......................... 55

Chapter 8: The Power of the Written Word 68

Chapter 9: What Does Self-Compassion Actually Mean? 70

Chapter 10: Why Everything Starts With Self-Acceptance 81

Chapter 11: Self-Love & What YOU Deserve... 89

Chapter 12: Importance of Achieving Emotional Balance 97

Chapter 13: Playing a Parts Reconciliation Game 106

Chapter 14: Mindfulness Practices & Relaxation Techniques 116

Chapter 15: Purpose Beats Passion When Pursuing Compassion 125

Chapter 16: Self-Compassionate Eating 133

Chapter 17: A Positive Mindset 146

Chapter 18: Confidence 164

Chapter 19: Strengths and weaknesses 174

Chapter 1: Self-Confidence

Built its Not Purchased Low self-esteem and a negative self-image impact everything, from how you think about your job as well as the manner in which you manage your relationships Bottom thing to consider? Success and happiness are the result of faith and confidence in your abilities.

Imagine waiting to be promoted at work for five decades. Your job responsibilities as well as your home pay check don't fit. After many attempts, you give up. It's a lie that you're not going to get the job. It's just not enough for you to be recognized in the workplace. Then, the spiral goes downwards pretty quickly. As you sink, you fall further into a black hole of unworthiness. Even when more lucrative chances arise and you are able to take them, you do not reach out for the opportunity. You feel that you're simply not good enough. Does this sound familiar? If yes, it's likely that you could benefit from more confidence in yourself. The book is on self-compassion that is true. However, to truly understand this topic, we must be talking about self-confidence, too.

The Origin of Self-Confidence

Confidence in yourself can mean many things to lots of individuals. It is essentially the enduring confidence and trust of your abilities. It's an inner state of mind which is a reflection of what we think as well as what we think and feel about the world around us. It differs from day-to-day from person to person, and from circumstance to.

The basic biology of life teaches that the DNA of our parents passes on to us at time when we are born. Therefore, we have none control over the colors of our hair, eyes, or our skin. The primary bone density and gender (strictly biologically talking) as well as even intelligence can be transmitted through chromosomally-transmitted genes! In all the inheritance items we receive when we are born, there's absolutely nothing in the science which suggests that we can also acquire the confidence of our parents. (This section is the one where my 7-year-old self always being bullied in high school rages.)

Steps to Building Confidence

Self-confidence isn't something learned (all TED talks be damned). Self-confidence is an attitude of having confidence in yourself. It's embracing your body and mind and settling with who you really are and trying to find a way to connect your self-image with the one you would like to be. There is no set of rigid and immutable rules to making the best version of you.

Before you bite your head off, there are some aspects that you can do to increase your self-confidence. However, it is important to realize that these suggestions are not worth anything if do not believe in yourself first.

In this article, we'll go over the steps to boost your self-confidence and image starting from the bottom.

Step One:Stop Beating Yourself Up

One of the primary reasons why we aren't confident is that we constantly criticize ourselves. The human tendency is when we make high-risk and unattainable targets for ourselves but only to see them fall in the way when we're done with the day. Because of some reason, we aren't aware of the advantages of setting smaller realistic targets. Making small-scale goals are an effective method to gain ground and create momentum.

You might be a person pleasing type who is able to get everything accomplished for others and not for yourself. Everybody is first which means that your personal desires in the background -or if they're being considered at all. Perhaps you're doing this to seek affection and love. However, in the end this doesn't work. As time you begin to get angry and feel a bit used.

Let me tell you a fact: "no" is not an untrue word! Your self-worth and confidence isn't should not depend upon the pedestal others place you on. The only one who gives an ounce of thought about your health is actually -- yourself!

Let's look at the situation of promotion. It is assumed that staying at the same job having the same compensation over the course of five years resulted in you feeling uninspired and depressed over your decision to pursue a career. In a state of complete suffocation from a deeply-rooted sense of inadequacy, that has been sustained over such a lengthy time period, now you offer yourself a bowl that is brimming with negative thinking and destructive feedback. Every spoon you think to yourself "Why would I even bother striving? It's not worth it! There's no way I can contribute anything worth mentioning or valuable to the table. In the event that I had, then I surely wouldn't be here today!"

A Different Picture

Think about what you would experience if you were to take time to take the time to take a moment to congratulate yourself on your back when you have small wins and gratitude? Would you be grateful for your reliable colleagues you've met throughout your career? or your dedication to work in spite of stagnation, when people in your job would have become lazy enough to be dismissed? If you develop an attitude of not allowing that negative voice in your head telling you there's no way to be good enough, you'll see something positive in every circumstance. It will be much easier for yourself. This state of relaxation and fluidity would permit you to spot opportunities that previously missed. It might be time to launch that exciting idea you've been contemplating. Perhaps it's time to start saving for that. Perhaps it's time to venture out of your comfort zone so that you're able to grow!

Let's take another look. You are blaming yourself for not being able to shed weight despite all your efforts. Then you keep saying to yourself, "I look like a beach whale." When you look at the weight you're putting on the scale and find it sad. You try the numbing diet that hasn't worked. Instead of changing the way you think about yourself as a beautiful person

You decide to pay attention to the news media. You accept their outdated aesthetics and make them your personal. You gaze longingly at the size 4 dress you know will get you a place on the front cover of Vogue -- if you could wear the dress. You begin to think that you aren't good enough for your body.

The other side of the coin is that it is possible to choose to remain confident about your appearance. It is possible to recognize the fact that losing weight is an ongoing process. This won't happen within a single day, in the same way like you weren't able to put onto the weight in one day. Don't be too hard on your self. It is okay to forgive yourself for the weight gain. Focus on your accomplishment of doing something, which matters.

Remember that this is a process that will determine whether you're bound to meet your weight reduction goals. Therefore, what you have to be doing is to love the person you are in the process of becoming the person you'd like to become. If you're unhappy in the beginning do you know what will happen after you reach that pointwhen you reach it? You'll look skinny. Also, you'll be the same miserable as prior to.

Step 2:Be Compassionate to Yourself

It's self-compassion that we're discussing It's crucial to clarify from the beginning the definition of what it means, as well as the things it isn't.

Like confidence, compassion is a broad term that means many things to many people. When it comes to compassion it is important to understand that you can see two aspects of the coinage. To begin with, compassion means being aware of the suffering of others -- their suffering and your own also. Another aspect of this is that you are actually taking a vow to alleviate the pain or to stop it altogether.

The simplest definition of compassion consists of concern and sympathy to the suffering and misfortune of other people. This is a feeling of joy that motivates us to give our best to help others or a listening ear an ear to cry on whenever others are experiencing their lowest. The act of compassion is proactively. Most people overlook the other aspect of compassion. They choose to feel sympathy, and doing little else.

Compassion is more than just having the ability to be "soft" and "nice" and feeling sad to someone else or yourself. Compassion is actively engaged. If you're feeling compassionate, you are motivated to take action for the pain of others (and yourself). It's true that you should take action to lessen your own suffering. The majority of pain is caused by listening to the negative dialogue of the internal critic in all of us, even the most seasoned.

It's possible that you thought you couldn't score well simply because you weren't smart or the teacher gave it to you. What can you do to improve your self-compassion? Maybe you can think that the sole reason why your score wasn't high enough is that you didn't do enough study and not simply because you're stupid.

The power of self-compassion is to help you recognize the struggles you face as an aspect of life and takes small actions towards improving yourself. These steps might include committment to better options for wellbeing, including taking additional courses and continuing your education or even gaining Bruce Lee abs. The next step is to deal with your cynicism, addiction, gluttony or any other issue which hinders you from enjoying your most fulfilling living.

To further show this, let's take Kevin's tale. Kevin is an entrepreneur who has made it big However, everyone would rather suck on lemons from a villa Franca lemons over having an hour spent at Kevin's table. Kevin was not always this way but he was a different person at times. The people from his childhood can attest to that fact at the very minimum. The world changed for him when he was fifteen. The loss of parents to a tragic car accident altered his life. In shock, he was unable to grieve for the loss of someone important to him. As it turned out, he was the epicenter of his own volcano. A lot of repressed anger and anger is a threat to anybody.

The process of developing self-compassion will not be just a matter of not noticing the issue or using substances to let it go, even for a couple of minutes. The only thing you can do is method or practice that can relieve you of pain since when it comes to it the feeling of pain can be felt within your head. Sorry to disappoint you, but Morpheus was correct in saying "there there isn't a spoon." There are times when the sound of cutlery that we hear can only be heard in the head.

Self-compassion, in the case of Kevin, will be acknowledging that grieving the loss of a loved one is human. It is important for him to recognize that it's good for him to grieve in this manner. To change things it is necessary to let go of something that which he was not able to control before. Kevin is required to get out of his comfort area and seek out expert help in overcoming his demons of the history, and then associate with those who are optimistic about life and the way of living.

The first chapter of this book has taught how important it is to build self-confidence, and why it (unfortunately) isn't something that we're born with. How we decide to build our confidence will go a great way towards empowering our bodies with the ability to confront challenges with a straight face and is essential for developing the development of a compassionate mind. Self-confidence and self-compassion are integral to help you tap into your strengths and find meaningful meaning in your the world, fight depression and anxiety, and enjoy general wellness.

When you've read the entire section, it's best to take time to take time to consider the significance of this passage for you, and the lessons you've learned thus far. If you're the type of person who has a notebook or diary, take note of what changes you're planning to make and the most important aspects you want to keep in mind. Take a moment to think about how this message resonates with the person you are.

Chapter 2: Grasping the Evolutionary Advantage

British clinician Paul Gilbert came up with "the compassionate mind method." Paul Gilbert explains the power of human compassion. Human brains have developed for interactions with others. We can display the many features of ourselves, in order to build bonds with various species.

Evolution, which is also known as "survival of the fittest" has helped us develop inventive ways of living to transfer our lives onto - - and secure - the future generation. However, evolution has given us a baffling defect: a brain was not designed by us as a result of being able to react in ways that we would have to prefer.

In order to manage the endless stream of events that resemble our British social calendar which is life, we've developed safeguards when we're at risk of being injured. In this section I'll assist you in understanding the way these systems of regulation in the brain function. So, you'll gain an honest, unfiltered appreciation of your own self, and you'll stop from self-flagellation and constant judgments about yourself and self-pity.

Emotional Regulation Systems

In his book Dr. Paul Gilbert surmised that we are a complex species with three distinct emotional control system. Dr. Gilbert says that negative experiences in our early years could alter the systems and make us vulnerable to criticism as well as feeling of shame. The systems he cites are:

The Threat System. It helps you identify and deal with dangers in the world.

The Drive and Resource Acquisition System. It helps you to be motivated towards resource acquisition as well as overall improvement.

The Contentment and Soothing System. It helps to balance and achieve a balance between the two other methods. This creates a feeling of satisfaction and happiness in your.

While distinct, these three systems interact together and depend on each other. The understanding of the complicated interplay between the three systems will give greater insight into your relationships with yourself and others in addition to methods to increase your confidence.

The Threat System

90 percent of people faced with negative news or good news, choose to listen to the news that is bad first. It's much easier to take rid of it. This is due to the fact that as human beings and as a species, we

possess a developed ability to recognize the dangers to us and our friends and family.

If we get information through our sensors, our threat system is our initial point of reference. Its task is to search for potential threats. It is based according to an "better safe than sorry" principle. It detects potential dangersome stimuli it then generates strong sensations that could be triggered by terror, fear, displeasure or any of the three.

It's pretty simple to show. What is your initial reaction being shocked to see a deadly snake show up in your yard? If you're not directly related to split tongues I'm sure you'd imagine how fast and far you'd run, or even how you can use a gun at it to eliminate. The threat system is activated.

Another example is the reaction when you get the letter from the university you desire to join. The first thing you feel is let down, overwhelmed by frustration or even angry. This is your mind's response to problems -- all of which are not the fault of you.

The system of threat is among of the brain's strongest system, and it is able to consume a significant amount of mental and physical energy. There are four major elements of this system of threat. Let's look at them in detail.

1. Overestimation Of Threat And Intolerance Of Uncertainty

Imagine you're walking along the path that is very lonely in the dark, when something grabs your attention. The system of threat is instantly activated. The response is a burst of emotions that direct your focus to the possible threat hidden in the darkness.

The brain says there's an intruder, criminal or perhaps an alleged serial murderer. In nine out of ten cases the time, it's just the alley cat or a stray animal and since your fear, flight or freeze reaction is on and you are unable to overlook the possibility of making a mistake. It's better to be safe rather than sorry? If this has happened your life a number of times then you're definitely not one of the scaredy cats. Your brain is programmed to respond in this manner. This is perfectly normal.

Some people's threat system functions over time. As a result, people are extremely vulnerable and highly secure. It is typically the case when someone has gone through traumatizing experiences during childhood, or the last few years. An excellent example is the fact that war veterans are plagued by flashbacks and nightmares from their time in the conflict zone and how victims of rape are more likely to be agitated whenever they're at a distance or encountering strangers who are in their environment.

2. Tendency to Overrule Positive Events

The threat system concentrates on the tendency to ignore or disregard positive emotions as well as feedback and other events. Instead, it opts to focus on the negative aspects.

If this happens, you concentrate on what might go wrong, rather than everything things that have gone well. Your focus is on anger and difficulties, instead of appreciation or strategies. When you are you are faced with an issue that is difficult.

Imagine giving an address to a crowd. Everyone is smiling and there is only one person at the back, who's looking to you from behind with a downcast eyes and a rather smug look. The brain is focused to that one person, and all you see within a crowded room filled with smiling faces and laughter is one face.

Your brows twitch. Then you become angry and anxious. It is difficult for you to be friendly with the individuals in your vicinity. You have no other options. There is no way to think about relationships or friendships in the future. All you have to think about is the individual with that smug expression sitting at the rear of the room. The brain has a tendency to ignore positive experiences to focus exclusively upon the negative.

3. Worry Wart Syndrome

The third part in the fear system, which causes you to constantly consider the negative. Imagine you're at the PTA gathering and everybody says nothing but positive things regarding your kid. It is a time to bask in the praise from other parents.

Then the next thing you know, a single parent comes into your home and tells you a grotesque incident that will make your child look unworthy to be praised in this manner. And then they push your body away and then walk off the front door. If you were asked about the day What do you recall about that day? The person you find disdainful that believes is not up to par respect for others is probably the first topic you discuss.

4. Handling The Emotional Pull From All Directions

As you reflect on the many elements of the threat system that we've examined so far, we will be able to see how they impact the way we behave. It's possible to ask yourself what to do if you're faced with sticky circumstances. How should you respond? How do you react?

Let's revisit the situation we sketched in the first chapter. You've been not promoted in all the time at your current place of work. Part of you is angered at the boss for this since you think "My boss isn't entitled to critique my job! He's not my boss!" Another part of your mind is frantic, thinking "Damn it! Not yet! My work hasn't been that impressive. Like usual."

Part of you is tempted to sign your resignation as you're only able to handle the amount of B.S. A different part of you is begging to weep and run away or even hang yourself. This inner conflict could cause us to sway in various directions. For the simple reason that, whether you like it or not you're dealing with many, many emotions that you must deal withthis is hilarious, since the mechanism is designed to help you deal with stress can be the exact cause you're about collapse and explode.

The process of navigating emotional turmoil is simpler to say than do, however it's not difficult. The amygdala -- which is the brain's security system is stimulated by the brain's threat system, which can create a feeling of insecurity as well as reduce our self-awareness, and self-confidence in stressful circumstances. It's crucial to identify the triggers that activate your system of threat, and to take measures to remain at peace rather than letting your emotions take over.

The Resource Acquisition, Drive and Motivation System is a system of motivation that has historical roots. The system drives us to things we'd like and want -- - or think we should have for survival and prosper. It's about food and shelter comfort territories, comfort, and even social status. The system was designed to aid you in keeping your focus on your goals and desires and keep the focus essential to attaining or reaching these goals.

The nucleus of accumbens -- an area in the basal forebrain, has a significant role to play in the process of determining rewards as well as the way that the brain process these. It's responsible for the release of two major neurotransmitters, dopamine and serotonin. Dopamine is a stimulant of the desire. Serotonin handles satiety. Neurotransmitters are the ones that control this system. If you accomplish what you want, you'll will feel very happy about getting the rewards due to the rush of dopamine you experience. Although the threat system functions to defend, the motivating driving force can lead to a reckless pursuit of objectives. Set goals and then achieve them to earn the satisfaction of being satisfied regardless of any harm that it may cause others or yourself over the long term.

The drive system can be described as having two extremes. It can lead to dependency and addiction (think alcohol, drugs, as well as unrequited love) as well as compulsive behavior. Another possibility is depression, stress and burnout when pursuing of objectives.

It's commonplace to see individuals who are constantly alternating between drives and threat system. They're balancing in a tightrope with emotions of fear and anxiety on the one hand while cravings and desires in the second. This can be exhausting. While playing this sport it is impossible to find a place for peace, pure joy and gratitude for all it is.

Imagine the excitement feeling you get when you're close to the last penny and someone offers you an enormous sum. It's difficult to take the smile from your eyes. It can make sleeping an unimportant thing in your list of priorities. It becomes a struggle to stay still. This is the drive system in action.

The Contentment and Soothing System

In reality, excessive use of these two techniques can cause despair, exhaustion, shame as well as stress. This can cause a huge effect on our mental health. There's no calm in both systems, as long as their usage is in harmony by the relaxation and contentment system. It is a system that lets us be content about ourselves, especially in times of chaos over us. A state of peace and tranquility is integral part of who we are regardless of whether we disregard it for pulling from the two other systems. It is as Rumi stated, "The wound is where the light is able to enter."

The system of soothing allows us to give comfort for ourselves as well as others. It is about being able to give and receive kindness and love from other people. It's about feeling what it is like to feel loved, welcomed with warmth and kindness and being and encouraged. The feeling of belonging. feel like you belong. The research shows that these kinds of behaviors and experience can reduce the impact of the threat system and the drive system. They can give the feeling of tranquility as well as security and peace. This system gets activated as soon as that a child feels the presence or aura of their primary source. It is due to the feeling of connection and belonging are the main concept behind the soothing and contentment system.

For many, however that are prone to this, their soothing systems are typically blocked completely such as those who have a past of emotional trauma or abandonment or those who frequently are disregarded. It's not unusual to encounter people who react by expressing hostility towards the warmth, intimacy, comfort as well as other emotional states that convey security and care. The reason for this is typically developmental history, or emotionally painful experiences for example, childhood experiences like humiliation, shame or rape, bullying parent hostility or indifferentness. When victims of these experiences receive care and warmness, it can cause a fear of harm and not security.

Brain Development and Its Ties to Evolution

When we are born, our brains comprise around 100 billion neurons, or neurons that expand by geometrically increasing. Every brain cell (or the brain cells) is home to approximately 2,500 connections within the neural pathways. When you reach the age of 3 it is estimated that there are 15,000 neural connections. When we are in our early years the number of neural connections we use increase, and those that are not utilized just degrade. That's Lamarck's Law of Use and Disuse at work. That is, "Use it or lose it."

When the neural signals that are that are strengthened have a connection by warmth, love and affection They help calm the nervous system. As we grow older the brain helps us feel and feel positive emotions as well as enables us to build connections.

In the event that this reverses during neural development and the threat system gets stronger, which makes it extremely difficult to come back from setbacks in our lives.

It's important to note two points. In the first place, if your system of soothing isn't fully developed this isn't always at the hands of the caregivers or parents, since children come with distinct personalities and capacities. Some children may not be willing to receive kisses and hugs however it doesn't make them less likely to create bonds.

The other thing to be aware of is that a poorly developed relaxing system isn't an indefinite fixture. This can be corrected by a little determination and expert assistance. Any time in our lives it is possible to make a deliberate decision to increase our happiness and calming system. This will help create a calm in the system of threat. It's all about creating and keep the harmony.

Neuroplasticity in Maintaining Balance

If you were to study an entirely new language and invest some time and effort in mastering it then your brain would develop as it should, doesn't it? Neuroplasticity is the capacity of the brain to create new connections on a regular basis. Similar to that If you want to increase or sustain your self-confidence level it is essential to put in the effort. By putting the effort into, as well as the brain's unending ability to build and reinforce neural pathways you can feel more confident about ourselves and boost the self-esteem of our clients.

The primary goal of this section was to introduce you to the components of our emotional regulation of the brain to help you be able to better understand yourself. The famous phrase of Aristotle affirms that knowing oneself is the first step to knowledge. What better way to begin to master your feelings?

Do you like the novel so far? If so, leave an a positive review. Go here for the page for reviews.

Chapter 3: The Role of Compassion and the Psychology of Shame

The trainers of elephants are able to make sure that elephants stay in one area. They pick the baby elephant and connect the animal to a tree large enough to secure the animal in position. After a certain amount of time the baby elephant realizes it isn't able to walk out of the trees. It is convinced that the tree isn't going to let it go -- even though it is able to actually remove the tree. This amazing phenomenon is known as learned helplessness and it doesn't just occur to elephants.

If you are convinced that the world operates in a certain manner and you accept it as fact, you can't doubt the truth of it. This becomes a part of your life. It's the same for shame. But don't be fooled by this. It's a human feeling. It's not the most pleasant sensation, but it acts as a reminder of when you've committed a moral unjust, and keeps your from repeating identical mistakes every time.

Once it's a strongly believed belief the idea that your character is inherently flawed, unworthy and not worthy the result is a completely entirely different kettle of fish. This is a form of an unnatural shame. Much of it's a result of your the environment you were raised in. The toxic shame makes you hide behind the bushes, hiding in fear that if you decided to show your true self it would be the end of the world to exist due to the zeal you bring to.

Shame: The Ugly Face of Beauty

Here's a wonderful quote from Salman Rushdie on shame: "Shame is just like anything else and if you accept it sufficient time and it will become an integral part of your furniture."

Do not think of the ironic name. Put it away from your thoughts. Have you had the pleasure of seeing an amethyst geode? Its sparkling crystals, with deep color that ranges from light lilac all the way to deep purple? Would you believe me when I say that they were once just a boring, sluggish fragment of hollow rock fashioned by hot lava? That gloom and sluggishness transformed into a dazzling piece in pure beauty that has therapeutic properties.

We are here to inform you that, as harmful as shame may be it is still possible to transform this emotion to help you find your way back. You just need some self-acceptance. It is important to understand that guilt and shame are a part of the essence of being an individual on a spiritual level. Understanding how it works can help you to accept it and then let go of the guilt. This makes it simpler to manage your feelings and expressing them is very easy. Shame doesn't need to be furniture. Throw it away.

Kinds of Shame

There are three types of shame. We'll discuss these three categories.

Reflected shame. That is what we experience when we witness the behavior of others. This could also refer to that others are embarrassed due to the actions we take. You may experience embarrassed when your child buys an item from a shop but you are aware that you're on a strict budget and are not able to afford the toy. A feeling of guilt or shame can be evident by the awkward look you provide to the cashier, even though you realize that the choices your child makes reflect on you.

Shame within. The shame you feel is reflected on your actions because the majority of times, even though other people might praise us, our opinion about ourselves is more negative. It is a form of shame that makes difficult for us to believe or accept genuine compliments. Someone tells you "Hey! Great top!" and the first you think will be "They say that just to make a point. The colour makes me appear dirty, don't you tell?" Internal shame is an element that weakens confidence in ourselves the most.

Shame on the outside. This type of shame is a result of the belief that the world is looking down on our actions. If you've gained some weight or are feeling bloated because of one cause or another. Then you start to believe people are judging the way you look because you've put on several pounds. It is then that you begin to dress more modestly and dress in baggy clothes since you think that others have a negative opinion of you but you aren't polite enough to point the issue.

External shame causes you to walk in a room feeling everybody is either praising your appearance or judging your face in a negative way. You end up believing nobody else than you. Different people use different ways for dealing with this kind of guilt. Certain people become more withdrawn. Some are more aggressive. You could say they're looking for fights once they see you.

External shame is a result of our human nature to be sociable since we are born with an instinctual need to feel valued, feel part of something and approval from others This is why it can be a painful experience when we feel disregarded in any way the eyes of others. How we handle the feeling of shame from outside depends on the level of self-confidence and our capacity to develop confidence within ourselves to take down any fear.

Six Types of Inner Critics

What are the best ways to make the most of forgiveness for yourself and practicing self-compassion while dealing with the inner critic in you? I think it's essential for you to understand your adversaries. In this way, you'll understand what to do to defeat the problem. If you are able to be able to recognize the negative voice inside your head more quickly you'll have the ability to let go and gain the capacity to show compassion. These are the 6 critiques we face every day:

The Underminer. The critic tries to convince you not to risk your life or try something new because you might be unsuccessful. The worry this critic is expressing is that you could be too strong, so it will try to protect you and keep you safe.

The Conformist attempts to stop people from identifying themselves by trying to conform you to an ideal mold. The

Conformist attacks you when you doubt the motives behind it, and then pours with praise when you fit in. It is always comparing your character to others. The biggest fear for this critic could be that the wild nature can leave you feeling lost and uneasy.

It's like the Guilt Tripper is as a vicious dog continually harping and berates the person for actions you've committed or did not do. The Guilt Tripper constantly brings up the past and those decisions you took that proved as unfavorable in conclusion. This is one of the most destructive because it does not allow you to to forgive yourself for your past mistakes. It's biggest worry is the possibility that you'll take a the chance of being at liberty and this will leave you without a conviction of obligation.

The Perfectionist. The perfectionist is a self-explanatory term. No task you undertake is flawless enough to be considered perfect. The program constantly tweaks and controls whatever that you design or the tasks that you take on. The stress of it makes you look as a skin. The greatest worry of the perfectionist is failing, as well as the rejection and judgment that are the consequences. It is easy to become stuck and not moving forward.

The Overachiever takes pleasure in the amount of effort it takes to complete anything even remotely. Although some call it hard work, strict rules for your life set from this type of critic can be described as a Molotov cocktail, ready to blow your life to pieces. This is a strict and authoritative system and has a set of standards for your lifestyle.

The Ass Kisser tastes as good like macaroons in the exterior However, it's deadly by making you concentrate on the other people around you, not you. Are you familiar with this? It's like you hear whispers in your head that say "Don't speak to her in any way. You might get her off if you decide to do. Maintain the current status. Keep it as is. Keep it nice and be friendly with everybody."

Taming Your Inner Critic

The thoughts you think about influence your mood and behaviour. If you are prone to self-deflection, you slowly take yourself down until you are left with nothing but your. If you are a victim of the voice telling you that you'll never be successful, and that you are of no worth, then you'll realize this to be the reality. It's that much more difficult to alter the situation in a positive direction or even accept your mistakes.

How do you get rid of the negativity that is going on inside your head?

Consider what tips you'd offer someone who is in the same position as you and treat yourself just as well the way you'd take care of them. Because you deserve it.

Imagine how disastrous the consequences would be if negative beliefs came to pass. This can go a long way in helping you manage difficult circumstances without having to deal with the typical roar of negative thoughts.

Stop worrying and ruminating over things you do not have control of, and instead spend on spending more time in tackling problems. Stay present, because it helps you.

Take note of your thoughts and realize that you think isn't always accurate.

Accept imperfections in yourself Acceptance is a balance with improvement.

Practice gratitude. It can give you a new outlook on the world.

Try to reduce the triggers that can cause self-doubt.

Practice mindfulness meditation and meditate. This is a way to invest in yourself and boosts your confidence in yourself. Meditation can be a gift that keeps going.

Self-confidence and self-compassion requires recognizing your mind's traps, recognizing your shortcomings, and building self-esteem by building a stronger self-esteem.

Internal criticism can be described as an attempt to disguise fear. Converting fear into confidence through acceptance of it will enable you to embrace the amazing present that you are.

Chapter 4: What Compassion Is Not

In previous chapters, I've explained self-compassion as well as outlined the reasons for why it is essential to the health of your body. With all the information you've learned the importance of self-compassion, it's important to clarify what self-compassion doesn't mean, as on this process of learning how to take care of yourself properly it is possible to misunderstand some things in the process. Therefore, let's clear details.

Self-compassion does not mean:

1. Self Esteem. Self-compassion as well as self-esteem can be two distinctly diverse, yet related notions. Self-esteem is a reference to self-esteem and the way we view and feel about yourself, self-compassion on contrary is dependent on self-reviews. Even if you don't, you'll agree that, in an effort to improve your self-esteem there are times when you display

self-centered behavior. We constantly put people down in order to feel better self-esteem. Studies have shown that self-compassion has a link to higher levels of emotional resilience and growth as compared to self-esteem. The story is short and sweet You can be a person with confidence in yourself and look like a pathetic excuse for an individual.

2. Self-Pity. Who would think self-pity or self-compassion can be close? It's absurd. In self-pity, you only whining and getting absorbed by your own troubles while forgetting other people are suffering from the same issues. There is no reason to think that to ignore the issues you face. The only thing I would ask is that you connect and get comfort by listening to others. You might even end up feeling better. In addition to the stress caused by being entirely in the midst of your own struggles and issues, you are finding it

more difficult to see the bigger picture of your problems, as you're in your personal psychological bubble. It is true that there is no problem in admitting that your suffering and being unsure about how you can handle the situation however, assuming a stoic mindset and waiting for taken care of leaves you vulnerable in the face of defeat and vulnerability.

3. Self-Indulgence. It's hilarious. It's the first day of the new job, so you receive a massive container of Ben and Jerry's for the congratulatory meal. You've just had a wonderful trip, and you think you should have a glass wine. It turns into a bottle. You decide "Screw it. It's probably better to take another." Self-compassion means you plan to spend less time in a hospital, and greater time enjoying a healthier lifestyle. Self-compassion is about giving your body the proper treatment, both mentally and physically. in other aspects.

Chapter 5: Mindset and Personal Growth

The term "mindset" has been first used during the 30's. Your mental state is the consequence of the way you've always been to think about the world. It is simply the belief system you believe in and your attitudes towards life and the beliefs you hold regarding life and the way they function, constitute your perspective.

Self-compassion is the reason why you desire to change your mentality, which is essential for improving yourself. It is simply because self-compassion can help you develop a perspective which is flexible instead of one that's fixed. This way, you can recognize the potential for development and growth where other people are able to see obstacles and failures.

The Nature of Mindsets

Mindsets are guided by a few fundamental principles:

Habit. The way you think is learned routine. It is a blank slate. with no traces. The way you develop your mind is through constant thinking about the world according to a particular method.

Bias. It doesn't matter if it is beneficial or not mental attitudes are usually bias. They don't necessarily create a precise picture of real-world reality.

Evolution. The way you think about yourself has the capability to evolve. This isn't a permanent aspect. It's a natural process that happens due to daily existence, and exposure to new perspectives as well as lifestyles that are different from the ones you're used to.

Chapter 6: Mindset as Binding to Compassion

Your mental state is at the core of who you truly are and it is your personal reality. There are three main kinds of mind-sets.

The Fixed Mindset Also called "the daily professional" If you're a person with a fixed mentality and believe that your skills have been fixed. It's not necessary to expand as there's nowhere for growth. If there's something outside of your comfort area or is beyond your perception, there's no way to know it exists Never, never will you be incorrect about anything.

The Benefit Mindset It is also known as "the everyday leader." If you are thinking this way generally, you'll seek to make a difference for yourself and those around you. It is important to look for situations that are win-win. If you're thinking about it what impact your actions affect others' lives is crucial. It is a question of why you choose to do the things we do and how others react with the same way. You make the right choices because of good reason.

The Growth Mindset. It is "the daily student." If you have a mindset of growth, you think that nothing can be made of the stone. If you're blessed with a talent or talent, as well as intelligence You believe that you can always improve. Everyone has areas places where they excel, as well as the areas they can do much better when they do extra effort.

Self-Compassion, Ambition, and Personal Growth

Many people worry that self-compassion stifles goals. The science suggests the opposite. Research has shown that people who are self-compassionate tend to be able to hold high standards of self-esteem as individuals who lack self-compassion. However, they're significantly less likely to feel self-critical for the times they fail to meet these standards.

The self-compassionate person is more inclined to commit themselves to the development of their lives than those who tend to be self-critical. If you have a mindset of growth developed through self-compassion, you're more likely to create particular plans to reach your goals while living an easier, more balanced lifestyle.

Attributes of a Growth Oriented Mindset

Take care of your wellbeing. It is the desire to lavish yourself and your loved ones with affection and a determination to confront a problem you're anxious about with a straight face since it's the best thing to act accordingly.

Sympathy. Sympathy is the ability to feel moved by your circumstances and be connected to the hurt you feel within you.

This is acknowledging the flaws in your character and accepting them.

Sensitivity. Sensitivity is the ability to be perceptual to emotions or pain that is felt by other individuals. Certain people are more sensitive in comparison to others, because they are capable of recognizing specific signals. They can radiate an aura of calm even during the storms.

Empathy. Although sympathy can be described as a felt feeling of sympathy or empathy towards someone else or yourself but empathy is a lot more. It lets you put yourself in another person's position to experience things deeper than if you were just feeling sympathies.

Chapter 7: Mindfulness

Mindfulness is the practice of taking note of events taking place in the world around your. It's a sense of an openness to events both inside and outside. The practice of mindfulness helps you be more optimistic, and experience lower levels of negative mood. There is no need to be a slave to the midst of anger, frustration or other negative emotions like you did when you are mindful. You'll be able to separate yourself from the flaws. This can help you create the feeling of safety and content. It may seem counterintuitive however it is the case for an extremely competitive society.

A lot of us believe that we have to appear like we have all the answers otherwise, people would be skeptical of our abilities and later criticize our abilities, and then judge us. If you're sincere with yourself, you know that the reverse is that is true.

Your flaws are your own. If you are trying to conceal your weaknesses, or to portray a perception that you're Achilles without heels the flaws you have worse for others. In addition, you'll become less aware of your real persona.

Exploring Mindfulness: the Johari Window

This section explains four primary kinds of self.

The hidden Self is the thing you can see within yourself that others do not. This is your self that which you hide from the the world in the name of protection, because it's the most vulnerable aspect of yourself.

The Blind Self refers to what you aren't able to see, however, others do see. The blind side might not be seen by those close to you due to fears of being offended by you. The self that is blind could reflect the best parts of yourself you question, such as beauty, intelligence or ability.

The Self you know is what you, and other people, perceive within the person you. It's the face of you which you and other people see and understand.

The Unknown Self is that aspect of you which neither you nor anyone else will ever discern. The Unknown Self could possess both beneficial and undesirable traits. In some cases, time and circumstance could reveal them, or you might die not being aware of what you're truly skilled at.

You are likely to be thinking "What worth do you think this window provide?" The Johari window can be used to help cultivate mindfulness because it is looking at the self and accepts it. The mind is a part of our own being. It's the art of making time and space, time to think, take a breath, and separate our own self and our reactions.

If you define your self or an object as being positive or negative, it is an assessment of value. Instead of continuously watching to determine what is good or bad, why not just take an extra step, release your judgment and observe what's happening and what might be? If you do this, you'll discover a greater significance to your the world around you. The self-compassion you feel for yourself will increase exponentially! You'll be more tolerant of you, too. This is an extremely positive aspect, since whether you whether you like it or not how you evaluate your peers is also the way that you evaluate yourself.

Practicing Mindfulness

It is possible to practice mindfulness wherever you want. It is not necessary to purchase any expensive items. All you have to do is dedicate at least a little time each day for yourself. Be aware that your mind is likely to be distracted, and practicing is the only way to stay your body and mind in harmony and fully present at the present moment.

Sometimes the brain goes through a short circuit and tries to fill the space by imagining an embarrassing incident that occurred at Christmas time, or your trash that you have to get rid of before the wife returns. or the old woman within your brain might think that it is time is the right time to engage in an honest self-reflection. What's important is to choose your reactions with care and let the "thoughts" be a thing of the past. Be aware of them, but remember that it is not your thoughts Your thoughts don't necessarily reflect reality.

There's no ideal way to be mindful. The key is to identify the rhythm that you are in. It's similar to dancing the Waltz. Once you've learned the steps, they will become part of you. It is okay to use them in everyday routines like taking a walk or walking your dog and even eating.

Mindful Exercises to Try

Mindful Breathing: It can be performed standing or sitting in a lotus position. Put on loose, comfy clothes and recline or sit in a chair. Close your eyes and breathe deeply through your nose and out through your lips which ought to be in a slight split. The focus should be only on your breathing. If you find your mind wandering -- and it is bound to occur -- don't berate yourself. Just be grateful that you were aware the distraction, and then slowly refocus your breathing. Do this. You only need 10-15 minutes a each day. Just 5 minutes can be enough to gain the benefits in a short time.

Mindful observation: This can help to connect you with the beauty around you.

This basically translates to, "stop to smell the roses." It allows you to see things you don't notice within the whirlwind of our modern lives. Choose an object that is natural from the immediate environment -- the smooth surface of a pebble, freshly cut blade of grass and a butterfly distant beauty objects that are out of you like the cloud as well as the moon. Take a moment to relax and immerse your attention in the moment for until your attention permits. Take a moment to look at the object that you have chosen as if you were experiencing it for the first time. Feel the natural energies it emits. It will be relaxing.

Mindful Appreciation: To achieve this to be a reality, all you're expected to do is look at five things throughout your life that you normally do not think about or appreciate. It could be items such as people, objects, or even phenomena. The purpose of this exercise is to express gratitude and acknowledge these minor items that you'd on an ordinary day, not give even a moment of thought. Try this exercise with a desire to strive for greater and more rewarding things. One example is the sweater you wear most often. Did you take a moment to appreciate the exquisite design? How would your life look in the absence of garments on your back that provide warmth during the winter months? After you've identified the five points, make notes in a notebook, or journal and reflect on what they mean to you as well as their significance and role within your own life.

Mindful Listening helps to let your ears be open to your surroundings and not be influenced by it as well as train your brain to not be influenced by negative thoughts and preconceived notions. Listen to calming music that you've previously not heard. The best way to accomplish this is by doing this with headphones. You can forget everything else and any thought you have about the style of music or about the performer. Simply immerse yourself in the magnificent beauty of music. Get lost in the experience of music. Relax your eyes and let your body be swept away by the sounds. Take note of the instrument and concentrate on the vocals in the sound, its range and tonal.

Mindful Insight: This practice assists you in achieving happiness with your present moment. It's goal is to move away the routine chores and constant stress that have become a regular element of your routine. Choose an activity that you engage in each day, like getting up the down stairs. Begin to feel and join the movement. Be aware of your muscles when they as they ascend or descend the steps. Take note of the space between each staircase and the structure. It is important to be imaginative and create fresh ways of experiencing the routine instead of slaving on the process.

Mindful Awareness: It helps to increase your awareness of everyday activities as well as the benefits they bring. You may find yourself doing something you don't really pay attention of, such as making coffee for instance. Relax and take in the way the perfect cup unfolds to you. Find your time to enjoy this moment. Recognize your hands and brain for helping you to get the perfect coffee Joe take place. I'm betting that, after this workout, your cup might taste differently. It'll be the most delicious coffee you've ever tasted -- each and each and every time.

While engaging in mindfulness, take note of your cues that don't require a physical the natural world. This could be that is as basic as the aroma of your favourite pasta sauce at home. If you get the scent consider how fortunate that you have the opportunity to cook an excellent meal that you can enjoy and enjoy with your friends and relatives. Pick a sound that you are able to connect with and periodically take time to stop and pay attention to the cues you receive and what they can serve in your life.

Common Obstacles That May Arise During Mindfulness Exercises

Images and thoughts that are recurring: It's normal to pay attention in the course of your exercise to be attracted to anything. There could be a specific sounds or notice something you're interested by out of the vantage point of your vision. There is a chance that you are thinking about a specific individual or event. If it gets increasingly difficult to focus on the issue and focus on the present moment, you should open your eyes and in this manner you're not trying to avoid the distraction, but rather acknowledging it. This is the real nature of mindfulness.

In the night, staying awake for meditation could be difficult task, since the calm never gets into your. In order to overcome this issue Try an alternative posture or stay off the bed, so you're not tempted give in to the temptations of Morpheus. Set up your own sleep routine and experiment by varying the times to do the exercises until you discover what is most effective for you.

Limitations on time: It could be very difficult to find time and time in your schedule to develop the habit of and meditation. Do not rush into it. I'd suggest you incorporate in it to your routine gradually, and then be patient with yourself during the times when you're busy or don't remember to take the time.

The mind-body connection: Mindfulness practices are a great way to uncover extremely strong emotions. Extreme emotions that are normally suppressed can be a means to come out at these times. You are fine when you feel these. There is nothing wrong with you. Every emotion wants to be experienced, even if it's more difficult to do take the time to be a part of the feeling instead of trying to hide it deeper.

Why Mindfulness Exercises?

The regular practice of mindful exercises can help to develop a conscious mind, which frees you from self-deprecating, naive thoughts and keeps you solidly rooted in positive emotions. This can help toward fostering compassion towards yourself as well as others.

Chapter 8: The Power of the Written Word

Writing to yourself can be an extremely effective form for therapy. It's not likely to disappear anytime nearer, according to my experience. It lets you communicate yourself in a manner that is impossible to communicate via a vocal communication.

Writing down your feelings on paper can provide you with the ability to release your emotions in a way which psychotherapy by a expert won't do. By using a pen and paper you'll discover a cost-effective method to build the connection between mind and body, shed emotional baggage, organize the emotions you feel and then tell your personal narrative. The story doesn't have to be flawless. There may be plenty of imperfections, yet be reflective of your feelings and thoughts.

How to Write Compassionate Letters to Yourself

Take some time, and then imagine that you've received a letter from a person who understands all your thoughts, and each and every emotion. Someone who has every negative thing about you but doesn't criticize your character for it. What does that letter appear to you?

Consider your top individual in the world. If they went through exactly the same thing as you're going through, what kind of letter do you think they would write about? Write this. After you've got everything down, you can end your piece with something which lets you know that it's fine to are feeling what you're feeling but that it's not necessary to feel the way you do.

Chapter 9: What Does Self-Compassion Actually Mean?

The term "compassion" can be understood as a compassion for others' misfortunes and pain. The emotion of compassion makes us understand and feel the suffering of those around us, and sympathize the situation of others. To be able to comprehend their difficulties without having to make assumptions or appear judgmental Self-compassion is simply the act of expressing the same emotions towards our own self. It's no more different than having compassion for the people around us.

Self-compassion is a way to become gentle with ourselves regardless of circumstances that aren't ideal. This can be challenging environmental circumstances we've been in or related to a particular aspect or that we do not like. This is about treating yourself with compassion in times of stress that is definitely more beneficial than being apathetic and sulking in self-critical thoughts.

We're not saying to be unaware of the circumstances you are in. Self-compassion recognizes the flaws of human beings. It helps us better connect with other people during periods of pain and loss. Additionally, mindfulness is promoted because it utilizes the present as an opportunity to be present and perceive things for what they truly are. Instead of suppressing our hurtful feelings or deflating them, mindfulness encourages us to be more present in our. Through self-compassion we have the ability to look at our circumstances with greater clarity and perspectives.

What Self-Compassion is not

While self-compassion means taking care of our own needs, many people believe it's self-centered, because we're focusing only on our needs. Yet, there is nothing more different. It may seem noble to prioritize other people but you won't be able to truly take care of others as long as you truly care for yourself. Be aware that being compassionate to us doesn't necessarily mean you're letting your self off the bill because of bad conduct. This is simply a way of accepting our shortcomings and mistakes with a manner that doesn't harm our self-esteem.

1. Self-compassion doesn't mean self-pity.

Self-pity is when we become so caught up by one's own issues, so that one is oblivious to the problems of others. Individuals who drowse themselves in self-pity often believe that they're the only one being afflicted in the present. This egocentric mindset typically exaggerates the gravity of their circumstances. It is common for them to get lost by the constant drama in their own lives. We've all met these kinds of individuals.

In contrast self-compassion can help individuals to face the personal experiences of their lives and mistakes with a greater sense of humour. They can see things from a bigger viewpoint.

2. Self-compassion is NOT self-indulgence

Self-compassion does not mean that you allow yourself to indulge in unacceptable behaviour. It's not meant to encourage selfish self-gratification that isn't earned, such as taking pleasure in unhealthy pursuits whenever you're feeling depressed. This isn't a pass-through for eating emotional food, lying about all day and consuming alcohol like.

We all require occasionally to feel a little cheery however, it is much more beneficial for our health to delay the pleasure for the bulk of. Self-indulgence usually focuses only on the present as well as the pleasures and comforts that make us feel more content at the moment. Self-compassion, however, inspires us to seek the growth we desire and make positive changes instead. It allows us to move forward when we are struggling however, without the necessity to feel guilty in the course.

3. Self-compassion IS NOT self-esteem.

We have talked about this in my earlier book, self-esteem is based on the self-esteem of a person and the perception of value. It is a gauge of our the appearance of our body in general. The self-esteem of a person is determined by our confidence as people. It's a result of our present successes and losses and how we rank on the pecking list of society. This is more of a personality quality, which means that the levels of self-esteem fluctuate depending on the changing conditions. If you've already read the prior edition of this psychological self-help book, there are likely to be some strategies to increase and sustain higher levels of self-worth in long-term.

Self-compassion, however, isn't a sign of competence it's a more profound and more generous feeling about oneself. Feeling genuine compassion for ourselves (and other people as well) is founded on the belief that all people deserve compassion, understanding and forgiveness regardless of their state of mind or position within the society.

There is nothing wrong with striving to improve your self-esteem. However, it could become a problem when we consciously create it as our primary source of satisfaction. When we are driven to do higher levels, we can inadvertently suffer and get caught into a perpetual cycle of self-criticism. It is good to know that being driven by self and finding peace within do not have to be two distinct things. Both of these can be accomplished through practicing self-compassion rather than being too focused on self-esteem.

The self-esteem focus is upon the negative or positive emotions you feel towards your self. Self-compassion is about accepting everything as it appears to be at the moment and accepting all feelings and thoughts associated with them and not defining anything as either right or wrong. This shifts the way in the way you view yourself in difficult situations, not a harsh, stern approach to being compassionate and compassionate.

Simply put, self-confidence will push us ahead in a self-critical way while self-compassion affirms that we're good in the present. It may seem contradictory however, to truly achieve peace and peace in your life, you must hold both these opposing concepts simultaneously in your head. They are both the right positions to be in which is essential to grow.

Being More Compassionate to Yourself

Individuals who have a difficult time taking care of themselves are often finding it difficult to build friendships. The way you treat yourself sets the tone for how others are going to treat you. If you aren't able to show yourself the respect deserves, odds are that you'll attract those that don't also have the capability to provide this to you. The seemingly unmanageable circumstances of life can be transformed by learning to not be so hard on your self. Below are some top amounts of ways you can do that:

1 Practice mindfulness

Mindfulness lets us be aware of the emotions we're experiencing and not be distracted by the constant whirlwind of thoughts that bogs down our daily thoughts . If we have to deal with our failings, it's easy to allow ourselves to get caught with self-criticism that it's easy to forget that we'll take it up again next time. It's well to listen to the opinions of our inner critic said, we must remind ourselves that the criticism doesn't make our character. Further details on how we can achieve this later.

2. You should treat yourself as you would treat your parent or someone who is suffering

A lot of us don't show kindness enough to ourselves, especially when we're suffering. In some way, we are prone to show more compassion and empathy when a family member or friend suffers pain. If we could learn to approach ourselves similarly with a sincere and calming manner it would allow us to look at our situation more effectively and in a beneficial way.

3. Be aware that you'ren't the only one.

Also, we are prone to believe that we're the only ones who've messed and making errors. The truth is that every person has their own amount of struggles in the world. Everybody is facing things that make us feel uncomfortable but we're not experiencing these issues for long. According to the old saying "this is also going to come to an end" which is why it's helpful for us to remind ourselves of that often to us. When we are more aware of our humanity as a whole and feel connected, the better we are to other people.

4. Accepting your mistakes

While we might encounter mistakes and bad experiences throughout our lives, we should not let them determine who we are. Avoid allowing those mistakes to prove that we're not capable to improve within time. If we can accept the fact that we're all human with flaws that are unique to each of us and weaknesses, the faster we will be able to figure out most effective ways to enhance our lives and our current mental state.

In the end, self-compassion doesn't demand for us to always see our self in a positive way to relieve anxiety, and neither will it lead us to the belief that we're more than other people to be happy. Self-compassion helps us feel more confident by offering an emotional security that allows us to feel at peace with who we feel. It is a requirement to discover how to feel confident in ourselves. Not because we're unique and exceptional, but rather because we're imperfect and that's acceptable.

Chapter 10: Why Everything Starts With Self-Acceptance

If we're aware whether or not we are aware, many of us engage in self-defeating ways and make us feel less satisfied. Self-criticism is often done in an unkind way as to constantly berate ourselves over the issues we think we've made mistakes. The voices of negativity in our heads are often so strong, they're the only ones that we hear. It's not necessary to explain the self-destructive nature of this and make an ideal life nearly impossible.

While we cannot always block those voices however, we are able to choose what we think about them and what thoughts we focus on. The good news is that we can. To better the health and well-being of us, as well as our mental health, it is necessary to look away from the judgements that we're receiving from people who surround us, and most importantly, from ourselves.

The goal is to reach a point in which self-acceptance becomes our normal state of mind.

Self-acceptance refers to the capacity to be able to accept all parts of you, all the good, neutral particularly the negatives. It is the ability to accept the body's image, ability to endure criticism as well as confidence that one's capabilities and abilities are a matter of. This isn't just about settling for your present situation. It's about pursuing the desire to be better and being confident that you're good adequate in this moment and present. It is usually simpler as you age however, the following suggestions can help to speed up this process over time:

Letting Go of Past Pains

We all be confronted with difficulties at various times in our lives. However, they will be to various degrees of intensity.

Nobody is invincible to suffering, it's an essential part of the human experience. Certain people learn to manage it more effectively than other people. However, the way you manage the inner pain will ultimately determine how you be and act throughout your entire life.

My experience is that it's really not the suffering the sufferers experience in these cases that is most traumatic. The real issue is the self-reflective guilt, and shame that we carry over the incident after the incident. In earlier books about how to fix this. This usually involves a revisiting of the situations for you to replay the events in your head. In the end, you must see these situations in a completely different way. Rewire your brain using positive anchoring, framing and framing methods that they do not hold a stranglehold over your mind. It can be extremely powerful and liberating after you've done.

This is not about denial of the reality of things or fooling yourself with the past. It's about giving more positive interpretations of events, and accepting the forgiveness you owe yourself for your previous, low consciousness blunders. Once we recognize these experiences as aspect of who we are and the person we decide to be and be able to accept ourselves as a whole. In this way, we finally begin to see the true value we have in ourselves.

In the moment we let go of the past hurts that we have endured We also release the obstacles that are preventing us from moving forward. This can help clear the way to a more positive perception of ourselves, when we let go of the unneeded expectations we've set for us. Create high expectations for yourself however, you should also give yourself a little slack when you're feeling tired, wounded and scared. You may also be angry, terrified, or unsure.

Opening Your Doors to New Opportunities

Accepting yourself is essential for true happiness regardless of where you're on the journey. The more you can show self-love you have, the happier you'll feel because you believe within your own heart that you're enough to experience pleasure. When you invest time and time to discover about what you enjoy and don't like about you acceptance of yourself becomes something which is innately yours. This knowledge about yourself is what helps you to overcome challenges.

Knowing yourself on a the deepest level will enable you to get the kind of jobs that allow you to realize your potential. The ones that can allow you to demonstrate to your world who you are truly made out of.

Every person has their individual strengths and talents that we could develop throughout our lives. Focus on those strengths and not our shortcomings. Develop these skills which helps to create positive feedback loops that are required for continued advancement.

Self-acceptance can be described as the master key to let you into many different doors. It can be an entry point to new places Many of them you believed were beyond your the reach of. It is easy to realize that you are able to do those things that you thought were not could be possible. However, more important is that you deserve the opportunities. This gives you the confidence to make the first steps toward your goals.

Learning to Accept Who You Are

This was a topic I addressed in the first few paragraphs of the book. However, the first step toward full self-acceptance lies in being aware of the person we really are. I've seen many struggle for a long time to please other people. Doing jobs that they dislike because they think it's socially acceptable to do it in order to satisfy parents with their demands like. But this shouldn't be done by all means in the interest of our own safety.

It's true that this can be a lot more difficult to say than do, and also that the smallest of struggles often have to be endured to bring about get to the bottom of it. But, it is important to develop the ability to change the cycle and finally recognize who you really are. Try not to appear like an extroverted salesperson if you're not. Don't be awoken in the next thirty years with a job or relationships you're not able to stand in the interest of others. This isn't just self-centered, but vital for the happiness of your own and the people that surround you.

Self-compassion is a battle which is fought mainly within yourself. It's a thing you have to take care of if you truly desire to bring about positive changes outside. Understanding yourself is about letting go of assumptions regarding the roles we're expected to perform, as well as the way we're supposed to act in the eyes of other people. It helps us have an open mind and let ourselves discover and discover who we truly are beyond the expectations that society has imposed on us.

Self-compassion and self-acceptance can help us accept the flaws and weaknesses to encourage us to be more mindful of our own needs. This is about letting yourself forgive your mistakes, while also transforming these into an opportunity to grow and develop. If we're able to acknowledge our humanness and love our own humanity without hesitation, then life becomes more logical when we are closer to the most authentic version of ourselves.

Chapter 11: Self-Love & What YOU Deserve

Do we look into an mirror, gaze in our eyes, and tell ourselves, "I love you"? You can bet you've never had the courage to do this. Also, it is likely that less people perform it without hesitation and declare the phrase out loud. As we spend our entire lives trying to get other people's love and interest, but we don't think about how crucial it is to put us first. As I'll be able to say throughout this book, it's the place the place where all of it begins.

It's not surprising that those who struggle to love themselves are likely to have a difficult time taking it on from another individual. A lack of self-love usually occurs when there is low self-compassion as well as self-acceptance. they're not mutually exclusive. In order to ensure that you have genuine and consistent self-love to become a reality it is essential to build your self-love foundations with self-compassion as well as complete self-acceptance. This article can assist you in this regard.

Why You Should Be Your Priority

Individuals who are struggling with self-love frequently feel that they are not worthy of anything because of the way they've been living their lives for so long. This can be due to repeated negative statements from relatives and friends that have been continuously added with time. The repeated criticisms do not constitute anything more than an elaborate story. The truth is that the perceived shortcomings we are describing should not be who we think us to be. The impact of words can be powerful and repeated use will increase their power.

It ensures that whatever that you put meaning on regardless of whether it's positive or not it will grow stronger. That's why self-compassion accepting yourself and your self become an answer, particularly if you've grown accustomed to feeling overwhelmed by negative thoughts and emotions. The Sufi poet and mystic Rumi often said "Your goal isn't to search for love, but to find and remove any barriers that you've constructed in opposition to it."

The power of you is to draw love from others through discovering comfort within yourself and your unique strengths and weaknesses, your current circumstances or even your past mistakes. The essence of love is only discovered in the moment we become the authentic and true person we can be. If you are able to truly love yourself the rest of your life will take a similar path. However, you must be the first priority for yourself.

The Self-Love and Confidence Building Process

In a society that is filled with many negative thoughts and judgements It will require a lot of work to restore confidence and that love we felt to our own self. It's not because we're unique, odd physical imperfections, emotional damaged. It's more that we've believed that our parts seem strange, insignificant and not attractive.

There's a lot is possible if just learn to accept yourself completely. If we can be proud of ourselves numerous doors will open to us. You can start the road towards self-love by allowing time for activities that we love doing as well as doing them without judgement. As an example, you could set aside a part of the day to engage in whatever you enjoy without guilt. It could include anything such as meditation, writing, reading or relaxing. Think of this as "me time" your moment to be completely relaxed.

This is also an excellent time to sit and think and consider your current capabilities and weaknesses. It is a good time to look back at your previous experiences, and then reminisce about moments when you thought that you had achieved something amazing. Also, you can relive the moments when you felt that you could benefit from a bit of improvement. It is important to determine the elements you could improve upon to improve your image of who you decide to be more in love with for the rest of your life. This differs from understanding your goals and achieving it, but we will discuss this in the future.

Enhancing Your Relationships All Around

It's difficult to stay engaged in a relationship if you're not loving yourself enough. Even though you and your partner can maintain your relationships for the moment however, the insecurities of your life will increase, and almost always causes disagreements. Sometime, these conflicts become intractable to an eventual divorce. This shouldn't happen.

But being able to show a healthy dose of self-love is a great way to enhance any love relationship. If the other person has also been working on their self-esteem and has achieved an elevated level of self-love. If two people are able to do this, their relationship is bound to prosper. Each person does not require one another to feel satisfied However, the combination of both parts makes that you feel more connected. That's how a genuine partnership should work, even though it isn't as popular these days.

If you're already married and self-love has become an issue this doesn't suggest that you should end your relationship with your spouse in order to resolve the problems that you are facing. But it can greatly aid if you get started on improving yourself immediately. If you and your partner have been battling with conflict caused by a inability to love yourself, you'll be amazed at the ways the situation can change as you see your strengths and trusting the positive aspects of yourself.

Self-love can be a process in progress as well as a lifelong work. It's among the main ingredients for maintaining happy, healthy, and tolerant relationships, regardless of whether they're platonic, family or professional. If you're feeling comfortable, confident and happy about yourself, you'll emit positive energy, which can be radiating. That is why the best people eventually become attracted to your personality.

Soon you will realize that being focused on yourself, specifically by practicing self-love, will significantly increase your quality of life. There isn't any greater reward to work to achieve. Now that we understand that it's crucial to develop a strong sense of self-compassion and love towards yourself, we can take action to improve it. In this regard, the next section of this book is focused on the methods and techniques to help you achieve that.

Chapter 12: Importance of Achieving Emotional Balance

The most crucial ways to go about first beginning to improve your self-compassion is to be aware of the state of your emotions generally. You should assess how you're experiencing in a day-to-day basis and to address the erratic emotions that result in the greatest distress. This can throw the balance regarding how you care for your self. Human beings are emotionally driven and regulating them can be a good idea generally.

We shouldn't suppress the feelings completely, but this bottled down or covering under the rug approach never will work long-term. The emotions will come out at some point, and it's wiser to be aware of these emotions whenever they occur. However, you can control the ways you react and to regulate your behavior and thoughts after when they have occurred. These techniques have been discussed in my previous books, but they're extremely relevant to an emotional balance discussion. That's why I've added the key concepts in this book.

1. Accepting your feelings

The very first step is become adept of recognizing and understanding your emotions. experiencing, and this is the place where the process begins. When I experience emotions arise in me, I make an instant to be aware of its presence. I sit for a while and experience it in order to identify it and put it into my brain. That's not exactly similar to taking action or reacting to the feeling however, I would like to be aware of the reason it might occur, and if it is useful for me. If I feel discontent, anxiety or anger I don't conceal or deny it, rather, I acknowledge it's there and deny it effective and then move on.

If you are prone to dwelling over these feelings and thoughts, you'll soon slide into a negative thinking process that will cause you to view everything in an unfavorable light prior to you realize it. It is very difficult to be compassion for anyone or anything in this situation. On the other hand, if it's an emotion that is a source of joy and joy or love I take a while, and acknowledge and write down what I'm feeling. I strive to create and use these times as these feelings are more favorable toward acceptance of myself.

It is also crucial to accept on the burden of these feelings whether they are whether they are positive or negative. It is a part of you that triggers the response you are experiencing, and you are the only one have to deal with it. It's usually the hardest step for some, however it is equally rewarding. It could be an external influences that have triggered this reaction at first But keep in mind that whatever emotions you're feeling originate from inside you and it's your job to manage these feelings.

2. You are not the only one who understands you. emotions

As a result of this, it is also important keep in mind that the feelings you experience from within, and the mind that interprets them are very distinct things. The majority of people are in somewhat of a wakeful sleep generally. They're in the hands of any thought, emotion or thought that pops up in their heads. Another good reason to evaluate the thoughts of others and directing your responses in the event that they occur.

Additionally, there is a significant egocentric element in this whole process.

The thoughts and emotions of stress or anxiety really are your own ego trying to hold your beliefs about the world. They are primarily focused to keep you in your comfort zone because it is believed to be the safest location to be. There is a need to discern between "thinker" and "feeler" with regard to this. Are negative emotions actually good for me? Are they ultimately creating self-defeating behaviour? It's most likely to be the latter.

3. Learn to forgive yourself and other people

Similar to the release of negative feeling that arises inside the person, there is an urge to keep the things they believe to be harmful actions toward themselves. It can cause harm in the event of an external influence that is a particular person or a group of individuals, maybe. But it's even more dangerous in the event that it is an act that we have made ourselves responsible for and must be forgiven. Remaining in this negative feeling will not be of any benefit for you in the near in the future, or for the long-term. "Holding on to anger is like taking poison and thinking that the person you are holding onto will end up dying" like the Buddha says.

If there's one aspect that made me progress within the world of business at such speed that was this idea. When I stopped throwing rocks at all dogs that were barking on the road, even myself, magic started to occur. I kept going regardless of how ill feelings I had in relation to a circumstance. The act of forgiving someone else has nothing that has to do with them however, it is all to do with the person you are. If you don't allow people to have a rent-free life in your mind, you're completely free to move on with your life.

4. Stay clear of self-talk that is negative.

Like I said earlier that letting self-talk about negative things become out of control is an awful habit. In my opinion, it's the single thing that afflicts humans more than any other. It is common for us to think we can get rid of issues before having the opportunity to begin them. This is due to letting negative thoughts or thoughts cloud our minds until we have there is no way out. It is imperative to stop this from happening as fast as you can to find a balance in your emotions.

It's not just about gossip and negative self-talk concerning the other person. If you are at risk of sounding similar to someone from your family or school instructors there's no need for me to explain that it's a waste of time that can eventually bring your awareness levels lower. There is no way to be perfect. simply make it a habit to notice whenever you begin to behave as you do. Meditation tips, later can be very helpful to deal with this.

It is also important to avoid being judgmental whenever you can. It really helped me tremendously as a person after I was able to quit doing this several years in the past. I didn't think of my self as one who judged others however, I did realize I was guilty of at times. By avoiding this, you is going to save you lots of time and energy. It is almost guaranteed that you will not every day, you will miss judging people.

These days, I just let other people get on with their lives with no of their actions. It's not to suggest that I don't tolerate bad behaviour nor do I try to analyze a person's character. We don't assess them in relation to what they did to arrive at the point they are at. I have never been into their shoes, or walked through the same struggles as they did and I have allow them to speak regarding this matter. I offer them some credit in the greatest extent possible. This is not to their advantage, but rather to protect my own mental well-being.

This is the essence of what it's about. If you apply these principles to your mental application, you'll eventually attain a more steady psychological condition. It will be easier to find balance in your thought process and greatly decrease stress levels throughout your day. It will help you rid your brain of the mental baggage you've been carrying around and make a place that is more suited to love and self-compassion.

Chapter 13: Playing a Parts Reconciliation Game

We have looked at ways we can distinguish the real us from the thoughts, we can achieve an emotional balance and be not judging. Another very efficient method of thinking that helps in resolving internal conflicts. This can help us advance more effectively in peace and harmony however, most important of all, you be healed from within and experience higher levels of self-compassion again.

The technique is able to eliminate differences between the inner thinking "parts". It may seem odd to think about, but human beings have a lot of voices inside our heads. Sometimes, they're discordant and hard to discern which to pay attention to. Many people are able to make a perception of this but are unable to distinguish between different voice of the other.

It is important to define precisely what I am referring to by this. There is a chance that you possess a formal (or office) "part" when you are working in the world of business, like. These individuals typically act according to a specific way that includes adhering an extremely high standard of social behavior and respect for coworkers. Carl Jung described this as our masks for the purpose of interacting effectively with others.

Additionally, you will have the family aspect (often an additional one for both parents). This could indicate that your mother was extremely rigid and required perfection from you. In the end, you may feel that you need to conduct yourself in a specific method to placate your mother. However the father could be more laid back. Someone you turn to for advice that is honest aren't judged too unfairly when you make a mistake.

There may be an entrepreneurial aspect in your brain, that could literally propel you into the right direction from time to time. You may be compelled to take on the next business idea. The same fitness component could bring you to your gym every day for a time. Additionally, you will have an internal development part that will likely be the reason for your taking this course.

However, you'll also have opposites to these positive voices. You'll have your fun-loving side that is in your head telling you that "you only live once in your life, take a trip and have fun because you'll regret it later in the future if you do not". And then there is that lazy side, who would like you to lie in a circle all day doing nothing. This is easy to put down all the time. But, it's hard to get rid of these discussions, since each one seems to be positive to some level.

How do you go to resolve these confusing messages that cause mental dissonance and anxiety? The first step is grab the pen and paper, and start writing on the main aspects that you believe influence your behavior and thoughts the most. Be as transparent as you possibly can. The most accurately you do this, the more effective the result is. In essence, you're talking to your self here. No one other person needs to be aware.

Write them down. your perfectionism part or your procrastination and your creativity part. your anxiety. Select the parts that have the greatest impact on your life the most significant way and the ones cause you the most stress. Take them apart and then ask them what value that they can bring to the table? What can they help you? Write these down in the process.

What can you do yourself to accomplish this?

Let's consider a scenario for a demonstration of the process. An individual in the early stages of adulthood may be surrounded by highly divergent parts. They attempt to put together who they are as a person. It could be the business or entrepreneurial component, and the fun or carefree portion, for example. This is not unusual to happen for individuals in their 20's.

They may think they need with the basics of their future career by climbing that corporate ladder. Another side could be wanting to exploring Europe. If you're like me, it could be similar, or any other mix of these examples However, you'll see the idea.

Next, you must have an exchange of parts. Let's continue using an example of a person at the beginning of their adulthood as if that's the case currently. Then, you'll need to position each of the parts that are in conflict into the palms of both hands. Then imagine what the two are as. It could be anything however it's a crucial action to make, since whatever you envision comes from your subconscious brain.

The entrepreneur may appear like a woman wearing an office suit and carrying a case of leather that is filled with vital documents just like a lawyer. The more fun-loving part could be a tiny child dressed in an oversized t-shirt sporting the cowboy hat while playing with a gun. It is also beneficial to connect any feelings that might arise from these aspects, when talking about them.

The next thing to do is take yourself into the shoes of one the pieces and truly think about what it is thinking. You can ask it to tell you what it's giving you and what its thoughts are about the opposing one on the reverse direction. There is a chance that the entrepreneurial side is looking to advance in life, and make plans for the coming years. They might suggest that you are not rushing to get the results as the greater benefits will be rewarded after. The brain may not like the enjoying part, feeling it is blocking advancement and wasting time.

Put yourself in the role of the fun-loving portion, find out what it's offering on the scene. This might mean that it does not want you to spend your life in a rut or not take the time to go out with your friends for a night of fun and such. If you "grow into" you will have plenty of time to engage in serious business into your 30's and 40's.

You will notice that each of these explanations is "positives" that is to say. The best thing to do is look at ideas from all sides that are framed with this perspective I.e. things that have the best interest of you in mind. A party just to have fun would not be beneficial, for example. But, ignoring the memory or even losing friends networking opportunities could be a sensible point.

It's time to have an open discussion to determine if it is possible to solve this ongoing conflict between those involved. Take a look at what each of them is doing to help you, and try to find a way to reach a consensus. While focusing on the previous scenario, the majority of people would think that the business aspect has the greatest benefits, and must be the first to hear.

However, this does not mean that the trade off can't be done. Keep in mind that we're striving for emotional harmony with our emotions. This is why your fun-loving side might be able to enjoy a social outing with your buddies for an evening every month for a chance to release some tension. In order to keep connections and friendships, try put off important leisure trip until you've met specific financial thresholds.

After you've come to some kind of agreement between both of the conflicting elements You should thank the two for their contribution and then bring your hands together and reuniting them to one another within you. The result you will see is that you begin to be more relaxed as well as less confused and confused than you had to be. This will provide the peace of mind which will allow you to be so easy to feel empathy towards yourself and other people.

If you are a person who is, it could be like the one that we've discussed. You could have something entirely distinct, and that's perfectly acceptable. The goal is to provide you with an understanding of what to expect. The best advice I can give you is to take a look at the aspects of yourself that create most pain and conflict.

Determine what they're and then discuss in depth the goals they have for you. If they are of some benefit to you, negotiate and incorporate these. If one of them turns out to be negative, or something that has no significance whatsoever, take it off. It is okay to make this decision. There aren't many of these components anymore, but once I did it was an euphoric sensation to let them go. I'd simply say, "thank you for being an integral part of me however, I don't have your opinion. I'm a self-loving person, and I'm going to let go".

Chapter 14: Mindfulness Practices & Relaxation Techniques

In the next few days, we'll be moving closer to creating a healthy environment to cultivate self-love and compassion in the mind. The goal is to feel less stressed and more calm and balanced. It's time to look into a different routine that could have an enormous positive effect on your mood when executed properly. There are those who believe that self-compassion is just being in awe of this moment. For mindfulness to be achieved, we should explore this concept more deeply.

There are those who believe that mindfulness and self-compassion can be considered inseparable because each is a moment that are pure and unrestrained. It is a time that we experience absolute acceptance of the thoughts, feelings, as well as bodily senses. In its pure form, we are one with the world. Nature does not worry about the past, or worry about the future. It's only a human food. It's just there, and no work is required and everything is done.

I often speak of the value and benefits of relaxing the mind. I believe it is crucial to attaining peace of mind, in addition to acceptance of oneself. So, this chapter offers a few practical guidelines about how you can do this successfully. No matter what your experience level, you have no prior experience in meditation or mindfulness learning. There's a need to start somewhere And any quantity of time spent practicing will benefit.

It is impossible to fully determine what will happen during your daily life However, you do have the ability to determine how you'll react to the events. The wise people are aware of this on an incredibly deep scale, and they practice restraining throughout their emotional reactions. The emotions we experience inside can be like the ticking time bomb in our bodies every now and then. We can, however, be able to stop them using appropriate strategies.

The exercises below are two techniques that have helped my development of an attitude of relaxation. They've brought me calmness that has brought peace for me, and has helped me develop an emotional environment for compassion to thrive. These are available to every one of us, so be sure to actively pursuing these methods in case you're still not practicing them. I'll assure you that these practices will definitely be worthwhile for the little time and effort you devote each day to them.

1. Relaxation Techniques

If you're dealing with or experiencing a moment of extreme emotional turmoil, taking a step into a calm state can prove highly helpful. Relaxation methods can also help when you are experiencing the first onset of the emotions as well as easing the anxiety and stress they may trigger to come back later. They also help create an overall feeling of wellbeing and ease of mind in the first location, which is ultimately the goal.

There are a variety of relaxation methods accessible to you. Simply, you need to know ways to manage your anxiety levels under control in a manageable and safe level. A certain amount of stress may be beneficial, provided it is properly channeled and used. It could serve as the motivation to take actions and development. The natural anxiety can assist us to prepare for the upcoming occasions where we have to do our top performance.

In general, however try to stay as calm as is possible. It is the best situation for effective decision-making since the rational parts of the brain aren't impeded due to increased sympathetic nervous system activation, which activates the "Fight or Fight" system. The result is a dramatic shift in the physiology of your. This will trigger a release of cortisol, a stress hormone which is a physiological consequence of anxiety.

Don't miss out on the chance to take a break whenever it is necessary. It is also helpful to keep worries to a minimum. unnecessary and ineffective thinking can lead to excessive anxiety. Exercise, breathing techniques as well as laughter therapy and various other methods are accessible to you. Develop a routine to relax. Your mind and body will appreciate this.

2. Mindfulness Practices

Like I said earlier that mindfulness can be defined as an awareness of the current moment. Originating from Buddhism It actually appears to be an odd statement initially. "Mindfulness" seems to suggest that your mind has been "full" with thoughts but that's not actually the situation. Simply, it means to calm the mind and to become completely aware of thoughts that do come up in a non-judgmental manner.

This concept of clear thinking has gained traction in all types of modern applications within the realms of psychology and the new modern self-help circles. This concept has been proved to be very effective at dealing with stressful circumstances in addition to the apex of emotions that these events can cause. If this is the case, feeling of compassion is a thing that's impossible.

This doesn't mean it will be easy initially. It wasn't easy to attain the state of complete mindfulness that is "No Mind" in the way I describe it. I could feel my brain being filled with endless and unnecessary chatter all through the whole day. I'd keep at it for hours in trying to silence it. If this is a familiar scenario then you're not the only one.

I'd say to myself "I am not going to leave this place until I keep a blank thought out of my mind for 20 minutes". This may sound as if it's a simple task however, I'm here to tell you that many people this isn't the case. The first time I tried it, I was able to hold a single thoughts for about 3-5 minutes. It took me nearly 20 minutes before I could be able to achieve this. Now I am able to attain the state of mind every time and even in a matter of minutes at a time.

How can you do this at home? In the first place, you need to focus on everything going on around you. All of the noises, sights and noises. Everything. The second thing is to be able to focus only on an aspect of the present moment, for instance breathing, so as to be able to engage in peaceful meditation. Most importantly ensure that you keep the focus of your current moment.

It's not a simple task to master however, once you master it the practice, it's an effective instrument. If you're finding it difficult beginning, get the assistance of experts to help aid you in your meditation training. There are a lot of great books about the subject in which you can learn about its techniques and benefits in greater depth than I will be able to present here. Therefore, my suggestion is to conduct your own research before you begin your journey of mindful living.

My favorite authors include Thich Nhat Hanh. He is a amazing Vietnamese monk who's teachings have inspired me as well as numerous others throughout the years. However, I also recommend Eckhart Tolle who is the writer of "The Power of the Now" to provide a more modern perspective on the world . Many view Tolle as a modern and esoteric self help guru. Many believe that he's one of the spiritual masters adept at transforming negative thought patterns that are prevalent in the West.

Chapter 15: Purpose Beats Passion When Pursuing Compassion

In the wake of having examined certain mental tools and techniques that one could employ to become more self-respectful However, there's one thing that surpasses them all. It is the rationale to do what we are doing. This is where our beliefs and beliefs are mostly derived from. It's about determining the purpose of your the world. There are those who believe that this is your real goal, while others will claim it as your true desire.

They may appear to be similar to the other, however there are subtle but distinct distinctions that can create a huge difference. The most common type of passion is self-centered. the purpose of it requires contributing. I'm not convinced that the most satisfying quality of human happiness, as well as a satisfaction is not derived from aiding others in the process.

Establishing a strong bond with the family, friends, and society all around. This is the top of Maslow's pyramid as well as the top of demands regarding self-actualization.

It is about doing things that you don't necessarily wish to accomplish, however usually, the actions that are the most essential for your development as well as personal growth. The goal is to fulfill our obligations and fulfilling our obligations, for the sake of building an improved society and society generally.

Passion, on the other hand is more individualized. It is a reflection of personal preferences and needs. This suggests that you only should be doing the things you enjoy to perform. It is, to me, naive at most. I am not a fan of just "doing the things you enjoy". It's true that we do not live in a time in which this can be done. There is a chance that we will live in a future prosperity and resource-based utopia where there is no need to be accomplished apart from the person who created it. The kind of time when days are full of walks through the woods, and not much more if one wants to.

But, I am convinced that it won't be enough to satisfy our fundamental human need to improve our own self-esteem, which usually results from aiding others in their growth. Leadership and responsibility are required. Also, I believe that you're susceptible to destroying your passion in the event that you decide to attempt to make an income out of it. If you are trying to make money out of your passion then you'll surely ruin what you cherish. Then you have to turn the product commercially feasible or to meet the deadlines for productivity of other companies.

It's crucial to understand the distinction between caring towards yourself and your passion for what you want to accomplish.

These are not the same thing. Through this book, I've stated that you must not be selfish at all times with regard to taking care for your self. This is the only way to give this same love to other people. However, this isn't what we're talking about today. The focus is on the outside performing actions we do on the planet. If we can find our true goal, then we're doing our best to be true to ourselves most of all.

This gives sense of security that can't be beat by anything else that you could achieve. This certainly beats the endless pursuit of the things you love all day with no regard to the bigger picture. The result is feelings of regret and anger as well as two methods to be less loving over the long term.

Societies Trick

It is easy to look at a few notable individuals within the society who managed to achieve fame by doing the things they love. They are however very few and far from the norm. These are the Madonna's of music, or the Serena Williams of sport. However, when you study them carefully, you will see that these people are able to demonstrate both their physical traits and determination to be a huge successes in their fields. If you've got the potential to be an elite athlete or musician and you are able to do it, by all means take it on. The reality is for every individual who signs a record contract or professional tennis deal, there are thousands of people who don't succeed to achieve it.

If you can find an opportunity for you to sell your skills and you have the skills that meet criteria to be considered world class take it. However, the best advice for the majority of people is to choose a subject that you're proficient in. It's something you're not completely averse to There are many people whom you can study from, until you're able to make a contribution your own contribution. Then you can pursue your interest or passion and be yourself, without feeling held back by financial pressures.

The issue is ultimately self-esteem and self-compassion. They are usually a sign of contests. They're activities of value that need to be compared with others so that you can see how you stand in relation to society. This isn't to say that they are necessarily bad. Confidence and competition definitely have a places within our daily lives. However, if you are seeking to attain an elevated level of self-acceptance you can find a different way. This method fosters compassion and companionship.

A Better Option

According to my experiences, you can accomplish this by trying to identify your goals. It's a worthwhile endeavor, but it's not an easy job. There is no way to stay in a dark space and contemplate until the thought comes to you. Sure, it'll be served by your mind's subconscious during some of your quieter times. While driving, or even during the shower, for example. It will require a lot of time and effort to think about it. It could take a few years or decades of experimenting with jobs or activities, career pathways and more. Certain people may discover the opportunity early when they are in their 20's. Some will discover it in midlife, around their 40's. In fact, many people will not realize it until after retirement!

It is important to being actively seeking it out. Engaging in the mental and physical job of knowing the purpose of your business. The majority of people try several business strategies or actions and feel dejected after they don't succeed with the ideas. If they don't get the outcomes they're looking to see immediately. They are mentally "beat down" and quit trying to find their real purpose. They don't realize is that the trial and error that they experience is essential to expanding, in addition to eliminating all items you do not like!

I believe that it's not a trip but rather a journey. That process must be properly navigated at every stage. It must be thoroughly explored before moving on to the next level. Imagine it as completing the level in an online game. In most cases, you must defeat a tough boss or difficult task for progress. each one more challenging than the one before. It's the same with life.

Chapter 16: Self-Compassionate Eating

It may sound strange from someone who is a psychologist, however I've included this chapter because I've discovered this subject to be extremely important and successful in creating positive effects in people's lives. My primary area of research throughout the years has included the areas of psychology. However, it is true that the body and mind can't be completely separated. When all systems are working harmoniously, all processes are operating perfectly and working in harmony.

It is also clear that it will be a difficult subject for some. Eating habits form over many years, and they can be among the hardest changes to make. Therefore, please bear with me and I'm not trying appear rude or condescending to any extent. However, rather, to present the things I've found to be the most beneficial nutrition-related tips for compassionate thinking.

Naturally, if you are suffering from pre-existing illnesses, it is recommended to consult with your doctor prior to changing your diet in any way. For the majority of us, it's important to return to eating healthy way. The way we were created to eat. This allows our bodies to heal and grow. This has had a major effect on the way I live my existence when I made needed changes in what I put onto my table.

Many would say that ethical eating is a full vegan. This is because we take other living creatures into consideration. This is a hard thing to argue with this. However, there is no moral declarations or assertions in this article. Just a simple nutritional approach to keep the body to function optimally. If you are able to do this, it's much simpler to get your brain to follow.

"Let the food be your medicine and medicines serve as your food"

(Hippocrates)

If you choose to eat in the form of an herbivore or omnivore generally speaking, the same principles be the same. It is time to shift to natural and clean source of food. It is important to focus on fresh fruits and vegetable aisles higher than we've been doing. Foundations for cancer research across the globe are continuously expanding the amount of antioxidants and vitamins from these food items, in order to fight off cancer. The typical daily intake is 10-13 servings right now!

An extensive and vibrant assortment of vegetables and fruits offers all the micronutrients we need to stay healthy. They provide the roughage and fiber for digestion aid greatly as well as being anti-inflammatory. A typical "Standard

American" diet doesn't include enough of these anti-inflammatory food ingredients. The first step is to correct.

In the next step, you must select appropriate sources of proteins, fats as well as carbohydrates to create your macronutrient balance perfect. The way you do this will be different depending on the fitness and health goals that you're trying to reach. In order to get healthy fats in the form of avocados with omega-3 content as well as nuts and seeds are essential. Lean poultry sources or wild caught fish is a must if you are consuming meat products. A diet high in quality, food items with low Glycemic Index (GI) carbohydrates in whole grains like brown rice, quinoa and plain oatmeal is essential.

Each of these sources of food provide sufficient energy and nutrients on their own. Each of them serves a role for energy production or the supply of nutrients.

Beware of "empty calories" food items on the other side is equally important in that they accomplish exactly the opposite. Sweets processed with sugar and other snacks provide little nutritional value, and raise blood sugar levels and then crash. The ideal scenario is to would like to maintain your blood sugar levels as steady as is possible, not getting excessively high, and also not low. It helps us avoid emotions and mood swings. adrenaline rollercoaster!

What can we do to achieve this? Stop our reliance on foods that are high in sugar and shift to lower GI entire foods. The GI scale reflects only the impact that carbohydrates in a particular food affects a person's blood sugar levels. In essence, the greater the number, the greater the speed at which sugars are reduced and added to the bloodstream, in reverse.

What is a Good Carbohydrate Source?

Fructose containing fresh fruit, vegetables, beans/legumes/lentils, unsweetened whole grains & cereals. They take longer to breakdown, typically necessitating the removal of seeds as an example to ensure they're less high in GI because of their nature in comparison to regular flour. Consume a lot of oats and the only ones that contain one ingredient. Oats! Do not buy instant versions that are packaged in small, packets with flavors, as they're stuffed with sweeteners and sugar.

As important it is important to determine the things we need to get out of. The items you need to get rid of from your cupboards and pantry in order to get rid of it. If you're confused as to the meaning of these are, and what these high GI foods, with high levels of added sugar food items are, it is best to take a examine the ingredients tab at the bottom of the package. In general the food that contains ingredients like syrup or 'ose in the last line must be removed! Dextrin, dextrin, maltodextrin and maltose. High-fructose corn syrup brown rice syrup refiner's syrup and carob syrup are major warning signs.

The first rule I follow is to avoid everything that is packaged or any other form in the first place. When you go grocery shopping, and then only buy natural whole foods into your shopping basket. It's basically anything that your grandparents would think of as food. This is the most expensive option However, it is important to choose what you want to focus on. The foods listed above offer a lot greater value regarding nutritional value in addition to being non-pesticide, which means better mood control as well as less irritation and inflammation of digestive systems.

Furthermore it is important to avoid sugar-laden, nutritious and dense snack foods that are high in calories. There are many people who say that like eating a small apple is just the same as eating a pack (2 cups) of Reese's Peanut Butter Cups, since both of them contain 21,5 grams of sugar. Although this might be technically correct however, they're missing completely. The chocolate bar candies, biscuits, and chocolate are merely empty calories. They're sugar that's refined with nothing else. Whole foods, on contrary include fresh fruits and vegetables are packed with beneficial micronutrients for health, including antioxidants, minerals, and vitamins. Additionally, they have essential roughage and fiber that aids digestion.

A Word on Beverages

One of the main ways to make improvements by trying to improve your food habits and eat in a healthier way by focusing on the drinks that you consume. There's a lot of hidden sugar present in a lot of our favorite drinks which can boost the calories we consume daily in the event that we do not take our precautions. The average individual should cut down on any sodas or high-carb sports drinks. Replace the drinks by any of the alternatives below, and you'll notice an immediate change in the way you feel.

Water!

Most people find that simply substituting every beverage they drink by drinking a glass of water could literally cut down on their consumption of sugar per day. Additionally, it will provide the user with a myriad of other health benefits like cleaner skin, more concentration, and better sleep to mention some. This is all derived through increased hydration levels. It is true that drinking water isn't always practical, since people need a certain degree of variation in terms of flavor.

Herbal, Green, Peppermint Tea

Herbal teas are easy on your stomach and have a great taste and can give you some caffeine boost your energy levels. Make sure not to go overboard with these. If you are getting tired or exhausted, especially in the afternoon, you can make an iced cup of your preferred tea that will help you get to get through the next dinner. It is important to drink this as you adjust to low or no drinks with sugar, since you might feel tired from low blood sugar levels at first. Chamomile tea is a fantastic relaxing effect on your body and mind, and is a favorite of my when I want to calm down.

Black Coffee

There's still some controversy about whether coffee is beneficial for the body or it isn't. According to my study its positive effects provides on the decrease of cortisol levels (via the production of crucial inhibitory enzymes) surpasses any possible adverse effects on adrenal glands. Therefore, if your herbal teas don't work for you, there is an additional ace up your back. This is the black coffee. It's been found to boost spirits and levels of energy all day long. Avoid sugary capuccinos and similar.

Other Drinks to Avoid

Fruit Juices in Cartons or Cans

Be cautious regarding juices. In contrast to fresh, natural juices, those that you purchase from the grocery store of your choice contain significant levels of refined sugars as well as sweeteners, preservatives and other ingredients in order to prolong their shelf-life. If you just take a review of the labels that are on the bottles You'll be amazed to discover that many have the same amount of sugar as full sugar sodas with regard to sugar levels! If weight-control is important to you and these beverages are a must, they need been drastically reduced.

Diet Drinks

Avoid "diet" drinks as well as "zero sugar" beverages since they have lots of artificial sweeteners such as (stevia) and aspartame. Both are nearly as harmful as the full-sugar alternatives. There is evidence that suggests they can even cause weight gain to the same extent compared to sugar-free alternatives, and as well as a possibility of increase in cancer risk.

I once drank Coke Zero as I thought I could get the high-caffeine content without calories. Now, I opt for herbal teas or black coffee when I need to energy boost. I suggest that doing similar. If you're familiar with these drinks and are looking to transition into the "diet" variant to begin with, do it. However, removing the drinks as soon as you are able to is the best choice to take.

This isn't intended to provide a snobby eating suggestions. A few high-level elements that I've found that give you the highest opportunity to stay good and healthy. If you are able to change these little things in your food habits, you'll probably sleep more comfortably and experience higher levels of energy throughout your day. Most importantly maintain a peaceful mind to allow for peace of mind. In the final day, self-compassion demands the use of both mental and physical effort in order to be effective. If you be a good therapist to your body then your mind will also be able to follow.

Chapter 17: A Positive Mindset

When you examine the lives of the most famous people of this planet, there is a common thread in all of them: a happy mental attitude. They faced the most difficult situations, yet they maintained their chins up and continued moving forward with an optimistic mindset.

However, this doesn't suggest that you'll never face difficult times or have no failures, as many successful individuals endure a thousand failed attempts to achieve their victory. The only thing we see is the surface, and don't consider that it's their failings that determine an individual's accomplishment.

What exactly is a happy mind?

Are you aware that all the things of this universe, including thoughts, can be considered energy particles? If you are positive and believe in the power of positive thinking, then the universe will reflect your thoughts and energy and provide you with a positive result. It is therefore crucial that you do not get caught in the downward spiral or self-doubting beliefs. Since what you think about is the self-fulfilling prophecy you have been putting in your head.

A positive mindset always thinks and imagines the most favorable result for every situation While a mind that is negative can only sink into depression and misery. The best way to explain this is through the following narrative:

Two wolves in

The story is about a man from the past who imparts to his grandson an important aspect about the world.

His grandson was asked, "There are two wolves inside us all and they're always in fight with one another. The one wolf symbolizes the best things about life, such as happiness and kindness, compassion faith, love and truth. The other wolf represents hatred, anger, hatred and despair. Which one will you choose to win?"

Confusionated, the child says, "I don't know grandfather who is the winner?"

The grandfather is graciously smiling at him, and then teaches him the most significant knowledge of his life. The one that will create and define his personality for the rest of his life.

"The one you feed your to your son."

The story is applicable to our attitudes. If we can feed our minds positive thoughts, we will overcome the top mountains of our lives. If we feed our negative part, we'll never reach anyplace in our lives.

Mental states that have been conditioned

It's not your fault when you develop negative thoughts. Parents, society, friends as well as the media all contribute to this. Each day, you hear that there is no way to accomplish or reach and eventually you believe that way for the rest of your lives. Your responsibility is to free yourself from the chains that hold you back from standardization and insanity.

The potential to control the mind's subconscious

The mind of a person is split in two parts which are conscious and unconscious. Although we only are aware of we think and feel while awake and conscious, our subconscious mind is constantly working and taking in everything. Psychologists try to assist individuals overcome their own views, they are constantly seeking to penetrate the subconscious mind levels.

The subconscious mind is extremely strong, and actually manages the conscious mind at the level of the surface. The deepest of our ideas, emotions, needs and worries are stored in this. So, even if attempt to suppress the thoughts or feelings be aware that it comes from your subconscious mind and will not be gone until you face the issue and attempt to solve the issue.

The subconscious mind doesn't stop operating and provides solutions for all your questions through tapping into its power. It is extremely robust and it is not able to alter the way it thinks by using willpower. Actually, it's the brain part which controls the conscious mind, so whatever thoughts or feelings you're experiencing right now, most likely, they originate from your subconscious mind.

Anything you experience at a conscious level is stored in your subconscious, even if you do not recall it.

To change your attitude, you must get to your center and begin taking good care of your unconscious because it is also the one that controls your body. That's why many develop ailments due to anxiety or stress. The constant thought of negative events or situations affects our bodies in a variety of ways.

If you are able to nurture your mental health (both conscious and subconsciously) you'll see an improvement on your daily life. Your mind will recover quickly and your mood will become improved and you'll be attracting many positive aspects to your life.

The Way to a Positive Mindset

Self-Acceptance

One of the first steps to having being a positive and healthy attitude is to be able to love you no matter who. You don't have to worry about which color your skin is or weight is since you're not only a small box is ascribed to the group you are part of. There is more to you than just that. You are able to climb mountains but, like the majority of people are, you struggle to climb a few hills. Therefore, don't be fooled into thinking that you're too... (insert the word "insecure" here) anxiety) to accomplish everything in your the world.

Be grateful for every bit of yourself, and then project that into the world to ensure that you receive the same as a reward. Give yourself the respect you deserve ahead of anyone else.

Practice Affirmations

It is an essential aspect of the process. Affirmations are the words and statements which one thinks, speaks or write about self for the purpose of educating your mind to be positive.

When we begin to believe that it is true, our mind will absorb the information as well.

Positive affirmations can be instrumental to build a more positive and stable mind. They are used every day in various forms, so they are ingrained in the mind of your.

Begin by stating a few positive thoughts about yourself and the way you live your life. It is possible to say them on the mirror, or record it in your journal. It's up to you, as the idea is that you are doing the same thing every single day.

E.g. You can affirm that "I have a fantastic life, and I'm able to do everything I like."

"I have beautiful features and have an amazing body."

"I cherish my family and my friends."

These are just a few examples. obviously you are able to customize your personal affirmations. It is possible to write affirmation quotes and place them in your mirror or workstation in the same way so your mind is reading it every day. Eventually, you will accept the idea. What we believe about is what we are. about.

Positive affirmations assist you in attracting everything are mentioned in them. It's similar to that of the Law of Attraction.

Practice Gratitude

A third essential element in a happy mental state is gratitude. It is important to feel grateful for the many things you've been blessed throughout your the world.

It could be anything from tiny and ordinary to the massive and intricate aspects of the world. Every thing happens because of reasons. What you feel now will become the joy that awaits you tomorrow. michel telo la boca

A break-up that you're devastated about could be preparing you to have a more fulfilling love life with a caring and loving individual. Being fired from your job could be a sign that there is a better job opportunity available to your.

The illness that you may be suffering from can be a sign to that you should be grateful for your health, and to help those that are suffering from the same condition. The way we react to what transpires in our lives is the ultimate consequence of our experiences that we experience in our lives. Therefore, in the end there is no failing only our choices or the thoughts we have about whatever occurs to us.

Everyone has their own challenges and demons to contend against. They're not trying to take us down, but rather to build us up and make us stronger and more brave. While it's not easy, you need to feel grateful. Only when you are grateful will positive changes in your life in ways you not have ever imagined.

Be around positive individuals

One of the most significant actions you can take is interact with more positive individuals. Establishing a supportive network to support you to work harder and helps to achieve your goals and dreams. Do not engage with negative or negative individuals who will only make you feel miserable.

If you're looking to form more friends, join various club or meet-up group and create new connections with similar individuals.

The research shows that those who lead a full and a healthy social life are less likely not to get sicker and do not suffer from depression Depression. Feeling isolated can be quite depressing, therefore you should always keep good people around you whom you get to know frequently.

Keep an eye on your thinking

The majority of the time individuals have their minds going through the motions and do not pay attention to the thoughts. It means that they have no barrier to stop negative thoughts, and it can be very easy to be enticed by the destructive cycle of negativity. Although it may seem difficult to keep a lid to your thoughts however after a few hours of practice, it is possible to become a mindful person as you think about issues. It is not the intention to suggest that you stop thinking or stifle your thoughts as this is almost impossible. However, it is possible to alter how you think about certain things as you look at or feel these things.

Find the positives in everything

There is no need to become the Pollyanna or pretend to be content when things aren't going your way. Your response must be to tackle every problem and addressing the issue. Then, things will begin to improve and change the direction they are heading.

Also, it is important to see the positive in people around you too. Make an effort to find the good within everyone, as this helps you to avoid any prejudices or beliefs regarding other people. Give others a compliment because it could be that you make the day of someone else's.

Positive energy is spread around

The most effective way to make yourself more positive is to share the word to others.

Research has shown that smiling causes the brain to release serotonin and endorphins (nuerochemicals) which help to calm the mind and body. Smiles are infectious, too and will trigger an immediate positive reaction 99.99 percent of the time when you smile to anyone.

Helping those less fortunate can make more you think about the blessings you have in your life, and make you more thankful.

Play with your pets and children. They are among one of the most adorable creatures which you are able to easily bring joy to. They will be able to experience the tiny pleasures that arise through playing.

Donate -- give things that you do not need to others who have. You could give away old clothes book, money or even books.

Meditate

The benefits of meditation have been demonstrated to alleviate anxiety and stress from individuals' lives. It isn't necessary to take a class in order to become proficient at practicing meditation. Meditation can be done in peace for as little as 10 minutes every time. Set the time set aside to rid your mind of anxieties and thoughts which make you feel worried or frustrated.

Relax deeply, and then close your eyes. Be mindful of being peaceful and content. When you begin doing the same thing regularly, you could perhaps boost duration and time of your practice and it will no longer seem awkward or odd to you.

Don't be a victim anymore, it's time to thrive!

Whatever you've experienced throughout your life, it's time to let it go and put aside the victimization card. If you are a positive person, even if you suffer from events, do not do nothing and blame the world or the world for what they've experienced.

It is possible to change your life for the better if you make the effort however, it can only be achieved when you are free of guilt and self-pity. Although it may sound harsh it is, no one enjoys a pity gathering. Some people might be hurt for you in a moment and may try to aid the person in need, but if all they notice is that you are wallowing throughout the time and doing nothing regarding it, they'll be more hesitant to feeling any guilt for them anymore. Make yourself an inspirational figure to others through your success in life, rather than just getting by.

J. K Rowling, the author of the hugely well-known Harry Potter books was a single, divorced mother to a tiny baby boy who lived in a filthy apartment located in one of the poorest regions in London. The author was rejected by 12 publishing houses, she did not quit and believed that she'd be published. In the end, she was accepted and, as we've all heard, the remainder of her story.

To forgive others

The final step in establishing positive attitudes is to be able to forgive others who have made mistakes, because no one can be perfect. The burden of feelings of resentment and anger over your experiences through the years burdens your life for a lifetime. The result is that you are stricken in a state of pain and frustration that it's impossible to live with peace of mind. The end of the day, forgiving someone is all about your sanity.

mind. So forgive them and get on with your life.

Being positive in your mind isn't that hard when you overcome these obstructions that stop the way for you. There is no way to be completely negatively oriented. It is important to keep an equilibrium with a focus on positive aspects.

Giving others forgiveness does not necessarily mean you agree with the things they have done to you, nor do you supporting any of their actions. This is just another way to heal from the pain the person has caused you. A lot of times, the reason why those who are unable to move forward in their lives because they don't have forgiveness for the individuals whom they wronged.

Chapter 18: Confidence

The world never gives a chance to the weak and fearful. The self-confident people who win in the end of the tunnel. It is essential to develop confidence in yourself and self-confidence to succeed in the world. Believing in yourself won't protect you from errors, but what it does help you to master is the capability to tackle every challenge through life with determination and confidence regardless of result.

There is no one born with complete confidence. This trait can be acquired from the outside stimuli that one encounters. If you are a person with an optimistic mindset, the confidence you have will grow tenfold.

It happens that your faith is shaken to the bone, but it shouldn't be the norm for a long time. situation.

What is the importance of confidence for the success of your business?

It is essential to be confident throughout your everyday life. From preparing for exams and interviewing for jobs to having dates with friends and making talks, being confident is the key for everything. Below are some reasons you need to develop confidence for your self.

Moves you

The confidence you gain from it makes you more active in your the world. It is easier to stay determined and certain of what you wish to accomplish, so you don't be unsure of yourself or inactive. Someone who isn't confident spends time time because of indecisiveness and fear of failure. It results in not taking action towards this goal and leads to the negative results. A person is then convinced that he/she will be destined to failing and the loop continues for a lifetime. An attitude of defeat can not just hinder the progress you make in life, but will also convince you that you're not worth any kind of success.

Helps you believe in yourself

The most confident people are the ones who first build their own emotional support system. It is essential to be confident that you can win on the field of the game of life. No matter if you have people saying that you cannot accomplish something, or if there were numerous failures you have had to endure.

"Whether you believe you are able to or think that it's impossible, you're correct"Henry Ford Henry Ford

Self-belief is a key component in developing one's character. If the world has you feeling down the one inner voice that is important the most. Keep that inner voice in check and don't let it go away. In many cases, it is our own self who guides us towards higher levels. So never lose faith that you are a powerful person.

Pushes your limits

Why set yourself up for failure to achieve more in your the world? An elevated self-esteem makes you increase your abilities to accomplish things you've never done before. It is not a problem whenever you try something different or new and you discover your own self-worth. When you test your limits to be successful The bar to be successful gets higher and higher, and your likelihood of achievement in your life increases rapidly.

It is a sign that you are saying yes to situations that you might have been hesitant to accept before.

Overcomes all fear

They also experience fears, however they never let their fears prevail and overcome them. Try to do one thing which scares you every day in order to help your confidence increase and you become completely fearless. It's not necessary to do to bungee jump or do anything terribly terrifying, however by making baby steps towards your goals, you'll be able to look your fear and let it disappear. E.g. engaging in conversation with a person at a gathering or asking someone to join you to dinner, delivering a speech etc.

How do you develop confidence in yourself

There are a myriad of ways you can try to increase your confidence levels increase dramatically. Here are some suggestions for you:

You can fake it until you have it

First step to boost your confidence is to take the path! It's not a matter of pretense or a fake appearance, the idea is emulation. Take note of the people who are confident and then try to replicate their behaviour patterns. The research shows that being confident and straight helps the brain develop confidence on its own. Before you know it you'll already being halfway there.

Test different ideas

Participate in various activities which will broaden your perspectives and ultimately boost your confidence in yourself. Also, this will help you uncover any talent you may have as well.

It could be cooking course, a new language, or even an entirely different sport. The more abilities and skills you possess and the better confident you are confident about yourself.

Visualization

"Whatever your mind can imagine and imagine, it is possible for the mind to achieve ."--Napoleon Hill

Make use of the art of visualization. Think of yourself as confident who can do whatever it is that you want in your life. Visualization can be an extremely effective tool to achieve achievement. The brain does not think about numbers or texts, instead, it thinks in pictures. If you can visualize something you'd like to do or behave in a specific way then your brain will recognize the idea and be more confident in your behavior.

Let your personality shine through.

Do not be shy about expressing your thoughts and emotions. This will help you to feel more confident and eliminate any shyness in you. Discuss with people different themes and topics around the globe. It will help you develop the ability to think critically and develop the ability to express your opinions. Explore other ways to express yourself including making art, writing or even building an object. There are countless ways to be yourself. Don't let your thoughts and feelings get bottled the thoughts and emotions in your head. A place to express yourself in a way that is authentic and fulfilling is the best option to build confidence in yourself.

Wear a dress that impresses

It is a bit of a shock to find out that dressing has a significant role to play in helping build self-confidence within the individual. Your attire can not just alter your perception regarding yourself, but people as well. A sloppy appearance makes you feel less appealing and decrease the self-confidence of others. Make yourself look good first, before aiming for other people.

The person who is well-dressed will always be viewed by admiration and respect. Whatever you're headed or whom you're with, present the most attractive person you can be and appear professional to everyone around you. It doesn't matter if it's an interview, party or a casual gathering with your friends If you've got an appropriate attire, you'll appear attractive to all.

Eye contact

Make sure to keep healthy eye contact with everyone whom you meet. There must be the proper balance of eye contact however. The eyes should be shifted to your sides each now and often to make sure you do not appear creepy looking into someone's eyes. Nor are you looking insecure or rude when you're not looking at someone's eyes.

You should equip yourself with the required information

Learn more about the different aspects of the world. So you can be confident that you're on the right track. Confidence and knowledge are inextricably linked and the more you are aware about something, the more certain that you're.

Do the things that you are passionate about.

Whatever it is that you are passionate about in your life, try to make it a routine to practice it each throughout the day. Engaging in activities you enjoy or enjoy can boost your confidence quickly. time.

Confuciusonce declared," Choose a job that you enjoy that you love, and you'll never be required to do a single day of work in your entire life."

Chapter 19: Strengths and weaknesses

Have all been born into the same world, each with its individual strengths, abilities and abilities. Similar to how each snowflake is unique, no two have identical patterns, ours is not like any other person. There are many different talents and passions that they're proficient in. When you are to compare yourself to others, it's important to know that you are unique and don't feel disappointed that someone else is better than your own.

Find your way to your success

Every person has their own way of living their the world. It is not necessary to run at the same track as everybody other because life isn't the same as a race against others, it's a race against the old version of you. All the time. That's why you need to grow and change as you go along with time and strive to be a more successful person than this week, last year or decade. However, it's difficult to do and we're constantly the same as our parents, siblings and classmates, or other people with similar ambitions and try to imitate the others. People who succeed don't copy other people or compare themselves to others and this is one of their main reasons for success.

Learn to identify your strengths

If you're honest or not, deep inside you are aware of what you would like to accomplish in your life, or the things you excel in. If you're not sure of the answer, it's your duty to discover the answer. You are responsible to yourself to discover the treasures that are that are hidden as talents and skills in your. This could range from an insignificant and arbitrary aspect to something that is extremely complex and complex, but regardless of what it is, it is important to find it.

Find out how to identify the right skills or talents?

Don't forget teachers, parents and other family members around you who have told you that you could or shouldn't be able to do something. They may have made their statements according to their personal opinion about your capabilities. It could be due to their beliefs or the differences in their thinking that led them to believe this way. If you believe that you are capable of doing something, take the initiative to do it. If you're not good at it, work on it and improve your abilities.

If you're still looking to find your own calling in life, you could consider these methods to discover what will suit you:

Register for classes at:

Writing

Writing is an art that does not come naturally to everyone, but anyone should attempt to learn. It's not necessary to be J.K. Rowling or write bestseller novels, but getting the knack of writing beautifully in words is something that you must know about. This is a valuable skill and something you can feel proud of. If you're not able to take classes in writing, then you must at the very least begin by reading books since one who reads regularly will automatically learn in the art of writing.

Write in your journal on anything that crosses your thoughts. Everything from your thoughts to day-to-day events and goals for the future It is a kind of therapeutic therapy to allow you to express your feelings. Journaling can be one of the greatest ways of expressing yourself as well as a great way for you to master how to write.

Learn to speak a different language

A new language is in a way that benefits anyone. It's a valuable capability to master the language of more than one and can also be used as a qualification in applying to different positions. In the end, you'll probably be able to be aware of a particular culture, and be immersed in the culture by studying it. Did you know that each time you are introduced to something new, such as the word "new" in a new language, the brain develops new neural pathways which make your mind more sharp and increase memory? This is among reasons that people who are polyglots are among the most intelligent people around the globe. If you're bilingual, it is still possible to master more languages to increase your knowledge base or gain your language skills. poor at.

Take a dip in the art of feet

Get started with sketching, painting or drawing. Learn sculpting or any other activity that lets you feel more expressive through aesthetics or the fine arts. The mind will get an outlet for creativity and will make you more efficient also. Go to art shows or galleries to broaden your understanding of various forms of art. This way you'll be able to determine whether you are a skilled or talents in this field.

Play a game

World champions begin their careers at a young old age, however that shouldn't hinder from determining the difference between a winner golfer or extremely skilled tennis player who is on the cusp of becoming. Explore different sports to see which one you're drawn to and excel at, and improve your skills based on that.

The benefits of exercise are felt on the mind, too and can help you feel the creative flow. It is possible to go to the gym for an enjoyable fitness session. The research shows that people who are physically active possess greater cognitive capacity and are more imaginative when it comes to their work.

Theatre

The point isn't to suggest that you shouldn't pursue acting, but you never know if it can bring out an ability you didn't think you had. Theatre or acting classes can make you more confident and articulate.

The world is yours

Try anything that makes you want to rise in the early morning. Perhaps it's a desire that you had in the midst of childhood due to being worried about failing or being told it was impossible to succeed. Be yourself and continue practicing until you are able to master the art of.

Important exercise

This is a crucial job you must complete in order to discover and limit the possibilities of the things you could excel at:

Note down all those things that you used be interested in or explored, always wanted to pursue and feel it is something you are able to achieve. Begin taking at least one of them each week, and observe what happens. Keep track of the aspects you are most excited about more than any other thing and the things you can do better or differently in comparison to other people. It may seem like an easy task, but if you do it right, it will benefit you for the future.

Weaknesses

Every person has their weaknesses, as well as their strengths. It's a reality that cannot be ignored. If you look at a success-oriented person and believe they have no flaws whatsoever, then you're incorrect. They have developed the ability to handle their weaknesses while leveraging their strengths. It's okay to be weak at something since nobody was born with strength or has diverse talents and abilities. You are just a tiny diamond.

Converting weaknesses into strengths

The world constantly pounds on our heads from childhood that we should focus on our shortcomings (not saying it's bad) but this should focus on your strengths, too. Our entire lives are spent focused on the things we don't have or don't have enough of, and we fail to think about what we are good at.

E.g. Zack isn't great at math however he is a great poet as well as short tales. However, his teachers and parents constantly tell him how awful his math skills are and that he's not able to advance through life if he does not perform well on math. In the end, he is discouraged believing that he's not capable of doing anything or thinks he's not clever enough. Sometimes, he stops writing poems.

Albert Einstein, once said, "Everybody is a genius. However, if you evaluate fish based on its capacity to climb trees then it'll live its entire life thinking it's dumb."

Accept your shortcomings

Many people who are seeking to achieve achievement are caught in this mindset of denial with regard to their shortcomings which is why they are more likely to fail. It is not a bad thing to start admitting your shortcomings. This will not reduce you to an individual by doing this.

When you recognize your weaknesses, it is simpler to work on your performance or get over it. Recognizing your weaknesses allows you make room to grow and also gives you an opportunity to improve and broaden your horizons.

You can be good enough at them.

In Zack's case, he was not a great math student, but this doesn't mean that it is a good idea to abandon math altogether to concentrate solely on his writing. The student should attend additional classes and study hard in order to earn an adequate grade. If you're afflicted by weaknesses does not necessarily mean that you should let it remain an issue for the rest of your life. Be able to overcome them if they're crucial to you Similar to Zack's situation since he was required to take the SATs.

www.ingramcontent.com/pod-product-compliance
Lightning Source LLC
Chambersburg PA
CBHW070557010526
44118CB00012B/1353